POWER BACK

A Bold, Soul-Shifting Guide to Healing
Trauma, Owning Your Energy, and Becoming
Who You Were Always Meant to Be

THE GLOW UP PROJECT

by MJ Grace

ISBN: 978-1-971349-41-1

Dedication

To every soul who believed in me before this was visible.

To the ones who held the vision when it was still forming.
Who listened to the late-night downloads, the rewrites, the doubts, the fire.
Who reminded me who I was when I momentarily forgot.

Some of you have walked with me my entire life.
You shaped me, stretched me, loved me through becoming.
Others were divinely appointed, arriving exactly when the mission needed breath.

To my parents, my siblings, and my friends, thank you for showing me that unconditional love still exists. Your belief gave me permission to believe in myself. Your steadiness became my foundation.

To She Rises Studios, Nadine Christine, Gio from The Love Change, and Steve Wallace, thank you for the long nights, the creative pushes, the honest conversations, and the relentless commitment to bringing The Glow Up Project and PowerBack to life. This movement carries your fingerprints.

This book was written by my hands, but it was built in community.

To everyone who has supported this mission, spoken life into it, invested in it, or stood beside me while it expanded, you are part of this frequency. You are part of this rise.

The glow is collective.
The power is shared.
And this is only the beginning.

With gratitude beyond words,
MJ

Table of Contents

Ignite Your Radiance

Hey, beautiful soul, let's set the world ablaze with your light.

Imagine us dancing under a sky bursting with stars, laughter echoing, hearts wide open, ready to unleash a revolution that's as fierce as it is joyful. Welcome to *Power Back*, not just a book but a cosmic invitation, a soul-led uprising, and a wild reclamation of everything you thought you had to hide. This book is about transforming your pain into power, creating the life of your dreams and turning your deepest aches into a wildfire of radiant possibility that no one, not even your past, can put out.

My name is MJ Grace, and I am your guide, part wise best friend, part therapist, part scientist, with a sprinkle of sass and a whole lot of heart. I'm here, healing my own quiet scars alongside you. My childhood, a tapestry of love woven with threads of self-doubt, taught me one truth: you don't need a catastrophe to feel the weight of the world.

You can grow up loved and *still* learn to shrink. You can laugh loudly and *still* carry invisible grief. You can show up every day and *still* not feel safe in your own skin.

And so, I'm still learning, still growing, still walking this path with you, not above you, not ahead of you, *with you*. I'm here to make you smile again, cry until your soul softens, and rise with a determination so fierce it makes the universe lean in and say, "Damn. They remembered."

As Audre Lorde said, "I am not free while any part of me is afraid."

Let's break those chains. Let's light you up. Let's call your power back.

Welcome...

This is *The Glow Up Project* , a movement I created to do something wildly revolutionary: unite your physical and spiritual selves for a healing so deep, so cellular, it rewires your nervous system, awakens your soul, and turns your timeline into a living miracle.

Power Back is the first written portal into this movement.

A guidebook. A manifesto. A call to remember who you were before the world told you to be smaller, quieter, more digestible.

It's not the whole movement, but it's the beginning. A foundation. A spark.

And you holding this book? That means you've already answered the call.

You are not just flesh and bone, you're a vibrant energy field. A divine spark wrapped in a human vessel. A multidimensional masterpiece, capable of turning wounds into wisdom, shame into sovereignty, and pain into poetry.

Energy is the golden thread that connects it all: your aching muscles, your spiraling thoughts, your intuitive nudges, your cosmic, "I just know."

When energy is blocked, you feel off, foggy, reactive, ungrounded. When it flows, you glow, babe, like a lighthouse cutting through the fog, like the answer to a prayer you didn't even know you whispered.

Mindfulness has been shown to help realign the nervous system and dramatically increase resilience, sometimes by 40% or more.

Translation: your body can heal. Your mind can rewire. Your spirit can roar back to life.

You'll notice a hummingbird graces the cover of this book, and butterflies appear often in these pages. That's no accident. The hummingbird has always felt like my mirror in motion: small but powerful, graceful yet fierce, defying limitations with speed, precision, and presence. It reminds me, and now you, that strength doesn't always roar. Sometimes, it hovers quietly, holding steady.

And the butterfly? Its metamorphosis is our metaphor: the journey from crawling to becoming, from hidden to seen. These two creatures reflect the heart of this work: movement, transformation, resilience, and freedom. Let them guide you as symbols of what's possible, because like you, they were made to fly.

What I'm Here to Do (And Why It Matters)

So what am I here to achieve? I'm here to light up your soul, to infuse you with a determination so fierce it could move mountains and melt self-doubt into stardust. I'm here to help you alchemize your pain, whether it's a quiet insecurity or a roaring wound, into power that radiates from your core.

Healing is serious business, but it doesn't have to feel like a funeral. It's empowering. It's creative. It's even fun, like throwing neon paint across a canvas and watching your masterpiece emerge.

I'm here to remind you who the hell you are:
A goddess. A king. A radiant warrior.
Not defined by what hurt you, but by what you rise to become.

As Toni Morrison said, "You wanna fly, you got to give up the shit that weighs you down."
This book is your wings. Let's soar.

The Sacred Union: Body + Soul

Your physical self, your body, your breath, your heartbeat, isn't just a temple. It's also a battleground, where stress, fear, and old wounds leave hidden imprints.

Your thoughts shape your chemistry:

- Stress floods your system with cortisol, keeping you wired and wary
- Love and connection spark oxytocin, building trust and ease
- Joy ignites dopamine, lighting your inner sky with hope

And then there's your spiritual self, your intuition, your divine connection, your inner flame, that never stopped burning, even when you forgot how to listen.

This is where *The Glow Up Project* lives.
Where muscles and miracles meet.
Where breathwork becomes a prayer.

Where healing isn't separate from science, it's the bridge that unites them.

Energy is the current flowing through your cells, your chakras, your nervous system, and your dreams. When it's blocked, life feels flat, heavy, disconnected. But when it moves freely, it *clicks*. You become alive, magnetic, unstoppable. You don't chase healing. You *become* it.

This Journey Is For *You*

This book isn't just for the brokenhearted or the burnout. It's for the achievers who still feel empty. The empaths who've forgotten how to shield. The survivors who are tired of surviving. It's for *you*, whether you're shaking off subtle doubts or clawing your way out of rock bottom.

Maybe you're tired of always having to prove yourself.
Maybe you're grieving something no one else saw.
Maybe you're healing from something that doesn't have a name.

The Glow Up Project doesn't care how loud or quiet your pain is. It meets you where you are. It sees what even you've forgotten to honor. It hands you tools backed by neuroscience, and practices rooted in ancient wisdom, because both matter.

Research shows that practices like breathwork, visualization, and energy-focused movement can regulate your hypothalamic-pituitary-adrenal axis (aka your stress command center), reducing inflammation, calming anxiety, and opening the body to healing.

But this isn't about erasing your past, it's about *rewriting what it means for your future.* As Carl Jung said, *"The privilege of a lifetime is to become who you truly are."* Let's claim that privilege like royalty reclaiming the throne.

What This Book Is (And What It's Not)

This book is your companion. A conversation, not a lecture. A love letter, not a listicle.

It's a heart-to-heart with me, someone who *gets it*. Someone who has been through the shame spiral, the freeze response, the fake-it-till-you-implode phase, yet decided to rise anyway.

We'll weave together:

- Neuroscience, to understand how your brain can rewire for joy
- Epigenetics, to show how your lineage lives in your cells
- Mystical wisdom, from Rumi to Goddard, to remind you that reality bends to belief
- Spiritual psychology, to teach you how to transmute pain into purpose
- Playful power, because healing doesn't have to be so damn serious

Visualization has been shown to significantly increase your chances of success, confirming what mystics, athletes, and high performers have known all along: your imagination isn't pretend. It's the architect of your becoming.

Think of this book as your own spiritual guide.
Each chapter is a step on the path.
Each ritual, a moment of return.
Each insight, a reflection of the wisdom already inside you.

This isn't a straight line, it's a spiral.
A journey of remembering, reclaiming, and rising.
Let it meet you where you are and walk with you as you become who you were always meant to be.

What's Waiting for You

This journey is a rebellion, a blazing, sacred, thunderous rebellion against everything that told you to dim yourself. A rebellion against every unspoken rule that kept you small, against every voice that told you, "You aren't enough."

What's waiting is not perfection.
It's alignment.

What's waiting is not control.
It's power.
What's waiting is the *you* you've always been, before the world tried to make you forget.

I'm here to help you laugh at life's absurdity, cry for what's been lost, and rise with a fire that can't be dimmed. This is your revolution, friend. A love letter to your inner child. A witness to your shadows. A scientific and spiritual map to radiance.

As Lalah Delia said, "She remembered who she was, and the game changed."
Let's change the game.
Let's ignite your soul.
Let's infuse you with determination.
Let's turn your pain into purpose so vibrant, the world can't help but glow with you.

What "Power Back" Really Means

You're here because, somewhere along the way, you lost your power. Not because you failed, but because you adapted. To chaos. To trauma. To being the strong one.
In this book, power means feeling safe in your body, trusting your intuition, setting real boundaries, and no longer shrinking to survive. It's about moving from autopilot to intention, regulating your nervous system, reclaiming your voice, and living a life that feels like yours.

I wrote this book as someone who's lived it, who broke generational cycles, rewired old patterns, and chose healing over hiding.

Power Back blends science, soul, and strategy to help you shift from surviving to thriving. You'll learn to calm your stress, alchemize your pain, and finally remember who you were before the world told you to be less.

This is your turning point.
Not a reinvention. A return.
Let's bring your power home.

The Battle Cry – Are You Really Ready to Rise?

This is your moment. The moment before the war begins. Before you step into the arena and face down every demon that ever whispered, *"You can't."* Before the pain you buried rises to the surface. Before the mirror gets real.

This book isn't soft. It's sacred. It's your *invitation to the underworld,* and your challenge to emerge sovereign.

Because healing? Healing is not for the faint of heart. It will not stroke your ego. It will not coddle your blame. It will not let you keep pretending.

It will break you open.

And if you let it, if you *truly* surrender, it will make you more powerful than you've ever been.

Ask Yourself Honestly: Do You *Really* Want to Heal?

I don't mean, "Do you want to feel better?" I don't mean "Do you want to stop crying, or attract a better relationship, or stop repeating the same toxic patterns?"

I mean this:

**Are you ready to face everything you've buried just to survive?
Are you ready to stop blaming and start reclaiming?
Are you ready to give up the story that your pain makes you special, and finally become whole?**

Because let's be real.

Some people don't want healing. They want *permission* to stay stuck. They want company in their misery, a comfortable cage where their wounds excuse their stagnation.

They want their trauma to be the reason they never have to rise.

They want their pain to be a plot point, something that defines them more than frees them.

You are not your trauma. It shaped you, yes, but it is not your name.

Your story isn't meant to be your prison. It's meant to be your *launchpad.*

So ask yourself again: are you ready to let go of the narrative that you've built your identity around? Are you willing to write a new one that doesn't make everyone else the villain and you the eternal victim?

Because if not, this book will feel like war. But if yes? It will set you on fire...in the best way.

This Path Is Brutal Before It's Beautiful

Ascension is not light beams and good vibes. It is the death of everything you thought you were. It is sobbing on the bathroom floor, then breathing deeper than you ever have before. It is isolation. Rebirth. Identity collapse. Liberation.

It is looking in the mirror and no longer recognizing yourself and choosing to love what you see anyway.

It is rewriting your nervous system. Reprogramming your subconscious. Facing your shame, your rage, your guilt, your grief, and *not turning away.*

You want peace? It comes after war.
You want joy? You'll have to meet your pain first.
You want to be your Higher Self? Then you're going to have to meet your lower self, and love them back to life.

Victimhood Is a Drug. Sobriety Is the First Step.

Let's talk straight. There's a seductive comfort in being the victim. You get to be right. You get to avoid risk. You get the sympathy. You get the story.

But the truth? The story starts owning you.

It becomes your identity. And when that happens, you start resisting the very thing you claim to want: freedom.

Healing demands accountability. It doesn't ask who hurt you, it asks what you're doing now to stop bleeding all over the people who didn't.

It asks:
- *Where have I abandoned myself?*
- *Where am I still seeking what I refuse to give myself?*
- *Am I willing to forgive, not for them, but for my own damn freedom?*

This work doesn't let you stay asleep. It calls you to rise.

Are You Ready to Rise *With* Others?

Here's another hard truth: if you're still secretly hoping others will fail so you can feel better about yourself, you're not healing, you're competing in the trauma Olympics.

Misery loves company, but *real power loves unity.*

Are you ready to celebrate someone else's glow without dimming your own? Are you ready to cheer instead of compare? Are you ready to be part of a rising collective, where healing is a ripple effect, not a solo trophy?

This isn't about one person winning. It's about *all of us rising.* We are not meant to climb over each other to heal, we are meant to *build the staircase together.*

So ask yourself: Am I ready to become a torchbearer? Not just for myself but for those still sitting in their own dark?

Because healing is contagious, but so is bitterness, and you have to decide which one you're going to spread.

This Book Is Not a Comfort Blanket, It's a Sword

You are about to go to battle. With your patterns. Your pain. Your illusions. You will face your inner child. Your shadow. Your false identities. The voice that tells you you will never be enough.

And then? You will rise.

Not as who you were. But as who you *really are.*

You will meet the self that was buried under years of masks and coping mechanisms. You will stand at the gates of your own freedom and whisper, *"I'm coming home."*

But only if you choose to.

Make the Vow

Before you turn the page, I want you to ask yourself.
Am I ready to face everything that healing will require of me?

Not just the journaling. Not just the baths and affirmations.
But the shadow work. The rage. The ego death. The forgiveness. The letting go of the story that made you feel safe in your suffering.

Because if you are,
If you're ready to not just read this book but *live it,*

Then make the vow.

Write it down.
Speak it aloud.
Feel it in your bones.

"I vow to face my pain.
I vow to reclaim my power.
I vow to rise, even if it breaks me first.
Because I am not here to survive, I am here to shine."

Welcome to the arena. Now put your armor on.

CHAPTER 1

What the Trauma?!

Let's be honest, the word *trauma* gets tossed around so much that it's easy to assume it only belongs to people in hospital dramas or war documentaries.

But trauma isn't just the headline moments.
It is the subtle ache you carry through a perfectly "normal" Tuesday. It is the whisper of *I'm not enough* that sneaks in while you're smiling in a photo. It's the quiet pact you made with yourself years ago to keep the peace by keeping yourself small.

I know, because I've carried it too, even after a childhood filled with love. This is proof that you don't need an obvious villain to leave a mark. Trauma can be born from what didn't happen just as much as what did: the love you didn't receive, the words you needed but never heard, the safety that was almost there but never consistent enough to rest in.

This chapter is about naming it. About turning to face what's been holding you hostage so you can finally start writing a new chapter, one where your worth isn't up for debate.

As Resmaa Menakem says, *"Trauma is a wordless story your body tells."* We are here to give that story a voice. To understand its roots. To tell it in a way that sets you free.

Redefining Trauma: The Weight That Moves In With You

Trauma is a shapeshifter. It doesn't always arrive like a hurricane, sometimes it seeps in like fog.

A hallway. Fluorescent lights hum. A circle of girls bent together, whispering. One looks up, scans me, and snickers. "She thinks she's

Studies estimate that over 70% of people worldwide carry some form of trauma. But most of us don't recognize it because we think trauma has to be big and loud to count.

Here's the truth: it's not always the car crash or the violent assault. Sometimes, it's the slow drip of *"You're too much"* or *"You'll never be enough."* It's the rules you never agreed to but followed anyway to hold onto love, safety, or approval. It's the years you've spent swallowing your truth because somewhere along the way, you learned it wasn't safe to speak.

Your nervous system doesn't measure trauma in headlines. It measures it in overwhelm, in the moments when you didn't have the resources, the safety, or the support to fully process what happened.

And here is where the science steps in: trauma rewires your brain. It hijacks and enlarges your amygdala, your internal alarm bell, and keeps you scanning for danger long after the threat has passed. You might find yourself bracing even in peaceful moments, as if joy is something that you have to earn. Trust feels like the monster in your closet waiting to jump out and attack, while safety feels like it's always one step away from disappearing.

That is not you being "overly sensitive." That is your body remembering.

Three Flavors of Trauma
(and Why They're All Real)

1. **Karmic wounds**—the eerie patterns that feel like déjà vu, always chasing love you have to convince, always losing your voice when you need it most.

2. **Generational wounds**—the pain you inherit without realizing
    it. Epigenetics shows trauma can change gene expression,
    passing hypervigilance or scarcity like an unwanted heirloom.
    Some of my own "too much-ness", too loud, too visible, wasn't
    mine to begin with. It was the echo of women who learned
    safety by shrinking.

3. **Current-life wounds**—the fresh ones. The breakup that
    fractured your voice. The rejection that confirmed your worst
    fear.

None of these three flavors of trauma are flaws, they are adaptations.
Survival strategies. They were necessary once, but just because they
kept you alive then doesn't mean they're helping you now.

*A drink handed to me by someone I trusted. A nervous laugh that
didn't sound like mine. The bright ceiling of an ER room. My body
became a courtroom where no one asked for my testimony. The story
my nervous system learned that night: trust is a trap.*

Naming them isn't reliving them. Naming them is reclaiming the pen.

Your Body: The Truth Teller

Here's the thing about trauma, your mind can explain it away, but
your body doesn't lie.

That knot in your gut when you walk into a certain room? That breath
you didn't know you were holding? That sudden tightness in your jaw?
Those are messages.

*A kitchen on a quiet Sunday. A plate clinks the wrong way and my
shoulders jump like a siren went off. Later, a joke, "Relax, I'm not
that serious", and my stomach roils because the punchline sounds
too much like the past. My body keeps tugging my sleeve: We've seen
this before. Please listen.*

Stephen Porges' Polyvagal Theory explains how your vagus nerve is the
switchboard for your nervous system, toggling between stress states
(fight, flight, freeze) and safety states (connection, calm). When

trauma is unprocessed, your body can get stuck in the stress setting. It's like a smoke alarm that won't stop wailing even after the fire's out.

But here's the best news you'll hear all day: it's not permanent.

Some studies have shown that mindfulness practices can reduce amygdala activity by up to 40%. Forty percent. That's not "woo-woo." That's your biology saying, "Thank you for listening."

And your body is a quick study. It responds to the smallest cues: slow, intentional breath; grounding touch; safe eye contact; movement that feels good instead of punishing.

You are not broken. You are brilliantly adaptive. You're just waiting for new instructions.

The Brain's Superpower: Neuroplasticity

If trauma rewires your brain, here's the plot twist: So can healing.

Neuroplasticity means that your brain can form new connections at any age. Yes, chronic stress can dim the prefrontal cortex, the part responsible for clear thinking and emotional regulation. That's why you might find yourself people-pleasing, numbing out, or sabotaging good things "just in case."

But every time you challenge an old belief, take a grounding breath, or speak up when you'd normally go silent, you're laying track for a new reality.

> *Therapist's office. My hands are fists in my lap. "You're not crazy," she says gently. "You're gaslit." The word drops like a key. Something inside me unlocks. That night, I make a new rule: I will not argue and defend myself against things that I know are untrue and not of me. I won't be gaslit anymore. I will not argue with anyone who requires me to abandon myself to be loved. My brain protests. My body exhales. The new path is muddy, terrifying, but it's mine. I whisper to myself "the kids and I will somehow be ok on our own..."*

At first, rewiring your brain is like machete-hacking through overgrowth. But over time, it becomes a clear road that you can walk in the dark. Healing isn't, "one morning I woke up fixed." It's hundreds of tiny rebellions against the old wiring, and each one counts.

Trauma Isn't Just Yours, It's in the Water

Here's a hard truth: Society is designed in ways that keep many of us in survival mode.

Hustle culture says, Don't stop.
Perfection culture says, Don't mess up.
Beauty culture says, Don't age, gain weight, or speak too loudly.

These aren't just bad ideas. They are nervous-system patterns, tiny traumas repeated until they feel normal.

And deeper still, systemic injustice, racism, ableism, sexism, and classism are not just social issues. They are ongoing nervous-system assaults that keep entire communities in hypervigilance.

But if pain is passed down, so is power. You carry the resilience of your ancestors, their survival skills, and their prayers. The same blood that remembers fear also remembers victory.

Why Naming This Matters

When you name trauma, you stop running from shadows. You flick on the light and realize that the snake in the corner was a stick all along.

This isn't about blame, it's about liberation. It's not about being fragile, it's about being fierce enough to feel.

As Rumi, a 13th-century mystic and poet, wrote, *"The wound is the place where the light enters you."* In other words: your pain isn't the end of your story. It's the portal to your power.

Your patterns (overworking, people-pleasing, choosing partners who can't meet you emotionally) aren't random, they're protection, but protection can become a prison.

Awareness is the key.

> *Living room floor. A journal open to a page I've avoided. I write, "I am not hard to love. I've just been practicing love in unsafe rooms." The tears that come are not collapse, they're release. My nervous system learns a new sentence: Safe love is allowed here.*

You don't need a tragic headline to justify your exhaustion. You don't need anyone's permission to claim healing. Your nervous system doesn't lie, and healing starts the moment you stop asking whether your pain "counts."

Your Turn:

Start the Conversation

Right now, take ten minutes with a pen and ask:

What's one moment or belief that feels heavy in my body?
Where do I feel it? Chest, gut, shoulders?
What might it be saying?

Don't edit. Don't analyze. Let your body speak.

Because this is where revolutions begin, not with giant leaps, but with a single, quiet decision to listen.

> *Wrist resting on paper. Breath low and steady. A sentence arrives that tastes like freedom. "I am allowed to outgrow the versions of me that kept me safe."*

And just like that, our story starts to change, and I'm honored to be on this journey with you.

CHAPTER 2

The Three Faces of Trauma – Karmic, Generational, Current

Your soul is a vast canvas, painted with the colors of your joys, your wounds, and the fierce spark that keeps you rising.

We've begun to name your pain, to hold it as a sacred thread in your story, but now we turn to face the beast that's been weaving those threads, a three-headed dragon called Trauma, with its Karmic, Generational, and Current faces. Each head roars with its own voice, shaping your heart's quiet beliefs, but none holds the pen to your story's ending. This chapter is your torch, lighting up these faces so you can see them clearly, laugh at their audacity, and finally write a future they don't get to touch.

With a fire of love in my soul, I invite you to meet this dragon, not to slay it but to tame it, and turn its strength into yours. Your trauma is not your master, it's the forge where your heart's fierce spark is shaped.

The Beast That Breathes Through Bloodlines and Breakups

Trauma is a cunning beast, a dragon that breathes its influence through your thoughts, your choices, your quiet moments of doubt. Its three heads, Karmic, Generational, and Current, each carry a distinct fire, yet they share the same body, rooted in your unconscious.

Trauma's impact isn't about melodrama or myth, it's neuroscience, epigenetics, and soul work braided together. These three faces aren't just poetic metaphors. They show up in your relationships, your patterns, your fears, and even in the ways that you flinch from joy.

This journey asks you to see each face, to understand its whispers, and to weave healing through small, fierce acts of love.

Karmic Trauma: The Echoes You Didn't Start, But Can End

Karmic Trauma feels like a cosmic script that you didn't sign up for. It's the inexplicable pull to chase unavailable love, to shrink your voice for no clear reason, or to have the sense that you're playing a role in a story you don't fully understand.

These are the echoes of lessons your soul carries, perhaps from beyond this life, whispering beliefs like, "I'm not worthy" or "I must prove myself." Think of Karmic Trauma as your heart's ancient riddle, nudging you to solve it. You might notice it in patterns, such as choosing partners who vanish or feeling small in moments of triumph.

Healing begins by seeing these loops not as curses, but as invitations. In a quiet moment, pause and ask, *"What is this pattern teaching me?"* Maybe you breathe deeply, picturing yourself stepping out of the loop, and choosing yourself first. You could write a single word (freedom, peace, worth) and let it anchor your day.

Mindfulness practices can quiet the mind's fear circuits, giving you space to rewrite these patterns. Over time, these acts, perhaps a daily affirmation or a moment of stillness, transform the Karmic script, turning its lessons into your soul's bold rewrite.

The idea of karmic trauma doesn't require belief in past lives. You can frame it as inherited soul wisdom, unfinished cycles, or unconscious archetypes. Whatever language you choose, the key is this: *You didn't start the story, but you have the power to end it differently.*

And maybe that's the real plot twist: You become the ancestor who breaks the pattern, wearing pajamas and drinking matcha, while transmuting lifetimes of pain.

Casual. Legendary.

Generational Trauma: The Ghosts in Your DNA

Generational trauma is the dragon's second head, carrying the echoes of your ancestors' battles in your very bones. It's the weight of their struggles, war, loss, silence, woven into your cells, which shapes how you carry stress or love. Your anxiety at midnight, your hesitation to rest, or your urge to apologize for existing might trace back to a great-grandparent's fight to survive, passed down like a family heirloom.

As Toni Morrison wrote, "You are your own stories and therefore free to imagine and experience what it means to be human."

You inherit not just their pain but their fire, their grit, and their unyielding will to rise.

Epigenetics, the science of how genes are turned on or off by life experiences, confirms what ancient cultures have always known: What your ancestors lived through shapes the chemistry of your body, your sense of safety, and your inherited nervous system. Their fears might whisper through you, but their strength is braided into your DNA, too.

This trauma shows up as beliefs like "I must always hustle" or "Love comes with sacrifice," which manifests as overworking or a fear of vulnerability. To heal, you honor your lineage while shedding its shadows. Close your eyes and breath, whisper, *"I carry your strength, not your pain."*

You might create a ritual, lighting a candle, naming an ancestor's courage, to release their burdens. Small acts, like resting without guilt or speaking your needs, break the cycle, weaving a new thread of freedom into your family's tapestry.

And sometimes, the most powerful ancestral work is this: *Saying no.*

No to over-functioning. No to silence. No to martyrdom disguised as duty. You don't have to carry their suffering to prove you belong to them. Your healing *is* your offering.

Current Trauma: The Wounds Still Breathing

Current trauma, the dragon's third head, is the fresh fire of your own life's battles, losses, betrayals, or moments that shook your world.

These wounds are raw, and you might start telling yourself, "The world is unsafe" or "I'm powerless."

Wounds can show up as a racing heart in quiet moments, a flinch at sudden sounds, or a struggle to trust. These are the scratches from your own adventures, still tender but not your whole story.

Healing asks you to hold these wounds with care, not to erase them but to soften their grip. In a moment of stillness, you might touch the ground, feel its steadiness, and say, *"I am here, and I am whole."* Build small anchors, a walk in nature, a warm cup in your hands, to remind your body it is safe.

Trauma is not weakness, it's your nervous system doing its job too well. You're not "too sensitive." You're too smart to ignore your body's alarms. Healing comes from teaching your system that it can rest now. You survived. It's safe to soften.

Over time, these acts (like breathing deeply or naming one thing you're grateful for) dissolve the belief that you're powerless, and instead show your heart that it can trust again.

You don't have to force forgiveness. You don't have to love what happened. But you do have the right to stop reliving it in your cells. Safety is a practice. Presence is a skill. You're already doing both.

Rewriting the Roar

Each face of this dragon, Karmic, Generational, Current, carries a lesson, a belief, a chance to grow. As mentioned, healing is not about slaying the beast but about taming it, using its fire to forge your strength.

You might start your day with a quiet moment, asking which face is speaking loudest, then offer it one act of love, a kind word, a deep breath, a moment of rest. If a belief like, "I'm not enough" rises, counter it with, "I am whole."

These small, fierce choices are your power, and your chance to direct your story.

Philosopher Hannah Arendt believed that action is not just behavior, but creation itself, the way we bring something new into the world. Arendt's vision reminds us that action is creation, and every moment that you choose healing, you're writing a new chapter for yourself. Your trauma is not your end, it's the forge where your heart's fierce spark takes shape; a light that burns brighter with every step.

And if your healing ever feels slow? Good. That means it's real. Fast healing is often dissociation in disguise. Real healing is messy, nonlinear, and gloriously alive.

You Are Not the Roar, You Are the Rewrite

You are not bound by the dragon's roar. Every time you face it, you claim your power and turn pain into possibility. Your healing is a bold rewrite, a refusal to let trauma define you, and a choice to craft a story of resilience.

You are the director, not an extra in someone else's tale.

The dragon isn't here to ruin you, it's here to remind you that your fire was never fragile. Now that you've seen its faces, you won't just survive, you'll *refine into something unshakable.*

CHAPTER 3

Unveiling the Shadows – The Three Core Types of Trauma

Imagine yourself like a tapestry, woven with threads of joy, pain, and everything in between. Each strand carries the weight of your journey.

So far, we've begun to name your pain, to hold it as a sacred part of you.

Now, we pause to look deeper, to unveil the shadows that linger in the quiet corners of your heart. Trauma is not a single note, it's a chorus, a trio of voices that shape your unconscious, and whisper beliefs that feel like truths.

These voices come from three core types of trauma, Developmental, Relational, and Shock, each leaving its mark, shaping how you love, trust, and move through the world.

This chapter is your guide to seeing these shadows clearly, understanding their roots, and beginning to heal them with a love so steady it feels like a long-awaited exhale. With a gentle fire in my soul, I invite you to explore these wounds, not to linger in their weight but to find the freedom they've been guarding. Remember, your shadows are not your chains, they are the keys to your deepest freedom.

Trauma Doesn't Knock, It Lives in the Walls

Trauma lives in the silent currents of your mind, guiding your choices before you even notice it. It's the flinch when someone raises their voice, the ache when you feel unseen, the racing heart in a moment of calm. It's the overreaction you don't understand, the shutdown you can't control, and the voice that says, "Don't trust this. Don't relax. It's not safe yet."

These are not weaknesses, they are the echoes of experiences that have carved deep beliefs into your soul, often before you could name them.

Your nervous system remembers what your conscious mind has learned to ignore. To heal is to hear these echoes, to hold them with kindness, and to rewrite their script with care.

Ancient healers, from the shamans of Mesopotamia to the oracles of Greece, knew that pain, when faced, becomes a guide. Nietzsche spoke of the will to power, not as conquest but as the drive to create meaning from suffering, to forge a self that rises through its wounds. That's what this is, a forging.

Your trauma is a call to that power, a chance to uncover the heart's silent script and write a new story of strength. Mindset and the strength to control your thoughts is the backbone of all healing.

And if you're wondering, "What if I don't know what my trauma is?" You don't have to remember the exact moment you experienced trauma to heal the wound. You just have to feel the impact. Trauma isn't defined by the event, it's defined by the imprint. And that imprint? It can be softened, rewritten, and transmuted.

Developmental Trauma: When the Roots Were Unwatered

Developmental trauma is the quiet ache of a childhood where your needs, for safety, love, being seen, went unmet, leaving whispers that linger long after. It's the young heart that learned, *"I am hard to love,"* or *"love is conditional, scary, or temporary,"* when the people and environments around you couldn't fully offer the warmth, safety, or presence you craved.

Most often, that wounding happens in relationships with caregivers, because of how attachment is formed, but it can also come from teachers who shamed you, peers who excluded you, systems that ignored you, or moments where you felt small, unseen, or emotionally alone. Developmental trauma isn't always loud, it can be subtle, chronic, and cumulative.

These beliefs, etched in your unconscious, show up as behaviors like people-pleasing, where you bend to others' needs to feel worthy, or perfectionism, where you chase flawlessness to prove your value. You might fear abandonment, cling tightly to love, or feel like an imposter and doubt your place no matter your success.

Developmental trauma doesn't always come from outright abuse or neglect. It can come from well-meaning parents who were emotionally unavailable. Maybe you were praised for achievements but not comforted in sadness. Perhaps you were taught early that your emotions were "too much." Or maybe you felt invisible in a classroom, or unsafe around the very people who were supposed to protect you. This kind of trauma teaches you to perform love, not receive it.

Healing developmental trauma is about turning toward your young heart with tenderness, asking what it needed then and offering it now. You might sit in a quiet moment, picture that child, and whisper, *"You are enough."* Create small rituals, savoring a warm drink, wrapping yourself in a blanket, to remind your heart it's safe to just be.

Over time, these simple acts rewrite the belief that your worth depends on others, teaching you that love begins within. You can start to say with confidence, *"I don't have to earn my worth. I was born with it."* And just like that, the roots start to rehydrate. Healing becomes a reparenting process, a sacred rebellion against emotional malnutrition.

Relational Trauma: When Love Came With Conditions

Relational trauma weaves its threads through the bonds that hurt you; the relationships (romantic, familial, or otherwise) that left you betrayed, neglected, or unseen. It's the wound of a parent's dismissal, a partner's betrayal, or a friend's abandonment that plants beliefs like "I must earn love" or "I'm safer hiding myself."

These show up as behaviors like trust issues, where you brace for betrayal, or hyper-independence, where you build walls to feel safe. You might shut down emotionally, avoid conflict because it feels like danger, or find yourself caught in cycles of toxic relationships, seeking love in places that echo old pain.

Relational trauma doesn't just hurt. It teaches. Unfortunately, it often teaches the wrong lessons: Don't trust anyone. Be perfect or be left. If you need too much, they'll leave.

To heal, you pause to notice these patterns, not with shame but with curiosity. You might ask yourself, "What am I protecting?" or write a few words about a hurt you've carried, letting them rest on the page. These small steps, done with patience, begin to unravel the belief that love must be earned, and show you that your heart is worthy just as it is.

And when the voice inside says, "They'll leave if you show your true self," you can lovingly respond, "Then let them. Because I will not abandon myself again."

Shock Trauma: When the Ground Vanished Beneath You

Shock trauma strikes like lightning, born from sudden, shattering events like accidents, violence, loss, or disasters, that shake your sense of safety. It leaves beliefs like "The world is not safe" or "Something bad is always coming," etched deep in your core.

These can manifest in reactions such as panic attacks, where your body braces for danger, or hypervigilance, where your eyes scan for threats even in peace. You might feel detached, as if floating outside yourself, or struggle to stay present, lost in memories of what broke you.

Shock trauma affects the body deeply, it's somatic. That means healing can't happen in the mind alone. You can't logic your way out of it. You have to *feel* your way to safety.

Healing this trauma asks you to ground yourself in the now, to remind your body it's safe. Try placing your hand on your heart, breathing slowly, feeling the warmth of your own touch. Notice the ground beneath you, the air around you, and say, "I am here." You may not believe it at first, but repeat it anyway, until presence becomes possible again.

Over time, you might create anchors (a favorite song, a soft scarf, a scent that you love) to bring you back to the present. These acts, woven into your days, soften the fear and teach your soul that safety can be found, even after the storm.

And no, healing won't always feel like a peaceful yoga session. Sometimes it feels like crawling through emotional mud. But even that crawling? That's movement. That's life. That's healing.

Healing: A Cartography of Courage

Healing these traumas (developmental, relational, shock) is not about erasing their marks but about listening to their lessons with love. Research shows that understanding your pain's roots can shift how your mind holds it, opening pathways to resilience.

Each trauma carries a belief, a behavior, a shadow, but also a seed of strength. You might begin your day by whispering to your inner child, "You are seen," or pause in the evening to name a fear, letting it soften in your breath. Build small habits, a walk to feel grounded, a note to yourself affirming your worth,that anchor your healing.

If a belief like "I'm too broken" rises, meet it with a quiet, "I am whole." These practices, done with care, are your soul's quiet map, guiding you from shadow to light.

Martin Heidegger, *a* 20th-century German philosopher best known for his influential work in existentialism and phenomenology, spoke of being as a dwelling in the world, a call to exist fully in your truth. Your traumas are not your end, they are the beginning of a journey to reclaim your heart, to live with a courage that transforms pain into power.

Think of healing like cartography, mapping your inner terrain. You're not getting rid of the mountains and valleys. You're just learning how to walk them barefoot, with grace. Maybe even with a little curiosity and badass glow.

Your Shadows Are the Doorway, Not the Lock

This chapter is my promise to you: Your shadows are not your prison but your path. Every moment you turn toward your pain, whether it's the ache of an unseen child, the wound of a broken bond, or the shock of a shattered moment, you're writing a new story.

Your healing is a spiral, circling back with new tenderness, each loop lifting you closer to wholeness. You are not your trauma, you are the light that shines through it, the soul that chooses to rise. Your shadows are not your chains, they are the doors to your deepest freedom.

Step into this work with love and patience, you're already unlocking your heart.

Your Turn:

Practice a five-minute "Heart's Quiet Map" ritual each day:

1. Sit in stillness
2. Breathe into your body
3. Choose one trauma to honor, developmental, relational, or shock
4. Whisper: "I see you, and I'm here."
5. Write one sentence after (e.g., *I felt my heart ease.*)

Do this for a week. Then add a small physical act, touch a tree, hold your own hand, say something kind aloud. Let that become your compass.

You're not just healing, you're returning to the self that never stopped existing in power beneath the ache.

CHAPTER 4

Healing the Hidden Self – Inner Child, Shadow, and Mirror Work

Within you lives a tender world, a quiet realm where your youngest self waits with wide eyes, your shadows hum a secret song, and your reflection whispers truths longing to be heard.

We've already named the potential sources of your pain and unveiled the traumas that echo in your unconscious, but now we turn to the sacred act of healing the hidden self. This chapter is your gentle invitation to cradle your inner child until they feel safe again, to embrace the shadows that you've tucked away, to meet your own gaze with love, and to let your soul's soft rebellion spill onto the page.

Inner child work, shadow work, mirror work, and journaling as a dialogue with the self are not just practices, they're a homecoming, a way to gather the scattered pieces of your heart and weave them into wholeness. With a fire of compassion in my soul, I offer you a journey through their ancient roots, their profound power, and the ways to weave them into your life, not as steps but as a flowing dance of love.

As I say in my *The Glow Up Project* community, "Your hidden self is not a scar to conceal, it's a sanctuary where your light is reborn."

The Inner Child: Where Innocence Still Waits

Your inner child is the softest part of you, the one who once reached for love, safety, and belonging, only to have those needs go unmet in ways that still linger. Long ago, in the temples of ancient Sumer, healers sang to the spirit's innocence, believing that nurturing the soul's earliest essence restored harmony. Inner child work is about returning to that young heart, the one who learned to whisper, "If I speak up, I'll be rejected," or "No one is coming for me," when the world felt cold or uncertain.

Working with your inner child is about creating a safe haven for that child, a space where they can rest without fear. Close your eyes and picture that younger you, small, vulnerable, waiting. Imagine holding them close, their small frame nestled against your heart, your arms a shield against the world. Kiss their forehead softly, look into their eyes, and say, "You are safe. I've got you. I'm sorry for the times you felt alone." Wipe their tears, and your own, letting the warmth of your love melt the old pain.

Kahlil Gibran once wrote, "Your children are not your children. They are the sons and daughters of Life's longing for itself." Your inner child is that longing, a piece of your soul yearning for care.

Each morning, you might sit quietly, picturing this embrace, whispering those words, or tucking a blanket around them in your mind's eye. Maybe you draw a picture of what safety feels like, a warm room, a soft song, or speak aloud, promising to protect your inner child always. These acts, woven gently into your days, re-parent your heart, teaching it that love is your birthright, that safety is yours to claim.

The truth is, most of us are walking adults with hearts still bruised by unmet needs. The world celebrates independence, but the soul whispers for re-connection. Inner child work is not weakness. It is radical self-reclamation. You become the person you once needed.

You say, "You are allowed to be soft here. You are allowed to need. I will never abandon you again."

The Shadow: Where Your Power Waits in Disguise

But there's another voice within us, often created from the tears of our inner child. A shadow that hums beneath our conscious thoughts, carrying the parts of us that we've hidden - anger, shame, fear, or desires we've deemed unworthy. Shadow work is the courageous act of listening to this hidden song; not to silence it but to let it sing.

In ancient Egypt, priests faced the underworld's darkness in rituals, seeing it as a path to wisdom. Your shadow holds beliefs like, "I must hide to be loved" or "I'm only worthy if I'm perfect." These beliefs were born from moments when you felt you had to shrink. To heal, you turn toward these parts with kindness, not judgment.

In a quiet moment, perhaps with a candle's glow, you might ask, "What are you protecting?" or "What do you need to feel seen?" If anger rises, breathe into its heat and notice its shape without pushing it away. You might write a letter to your shame, thank it for guarding you, or speak its name aloud and let it soften in the air.

Audre Lorde said, *"The master's tools will never dismantle the master's house."* Your shadow is not a tool to destroy but a house to explore and renovate, a space where every feeling, once embraced, becomes a beautiful new room to decorate

You may need to knock down a few walls, but that expansion creates a space for you to live with openness and flow and a lot more light.

What do you want your home, your soul, to look like?

Over time, this practice (perhaps a nightly reflection or a walk where you name what's hidden) transforms your shadows into allies. By threading their strength into your psyche, you're allowing yourself to meet life with more honesty, confidence, and emotional power.

You will learn that your anger is often your boundary's final line of defense. Your shame is a compass, pointing to forgotten desires. Your jealousy is the part of you still waiting to be witnessed. The parts of you that you've labeled "too much" or "too dark" are often the exact parts containing your greatest capacity for transformation.

We all have shadows, those quiet extensions of ourselves that appear most clearly when we allow the light to touch us.
They move with us, mimic us, but they are not who we are.
They are reflections, not definitions.
Distorted, yes, but never dangerous on their own.

Shadow work is the art of shifting perspective.
When you stop running from the parts of you that feel uncomfortable, and instead turn toward them with curiosity, everything changes. You

may not be able to escape them, but you can control them.
What once felt like a threat becomes something to learn from. What once loomed large begins to shrink in the clarity of your awareness.

My invitation is this:
See your shadows for what they are, feedback, echoes, reminders.

In time, you may even smile when you notice them, not because they're gone, but because you've reclaimed your power to choose how you see them. Be playful, laugh at yourself, notice the way you can manipulate them into a different shape.

You are not your shadow.
You are the one with the perspective to meet it, understand it, and walk forward, whole.

Mirror Work: Meeting the Gaze of the Divine

Then there's the mirror work, a portal to your own soul, asking you to meet yourself with unwavering love. In ancient India, reflective pools were sacred spaces for glimpsing the divine within, a truth that lives in your own gaze. Mirror work is about standing before your reflection, not to critique but to cherish, to see the heart that's carried you through storms.

Studies show that speaking kindly to yourself fosters a sense of worth, rewiring the mind to counter trauma's lies. Each day, perhaps in the dawn's soft light, look into your eyes and say, "You are amazing. I love you." Feel the discomfort, the urge to turn away, and stay anyway, letting your gaze soften like a friend's. Wipe a tear if it falls, yours or the reflection's, and smile, even faintly.

You might add words like "You are worthy" or "You are safe." Let them sink into your bones. Thich Nhat Hanh taught, *"To love is to be there."* To stand before your mirror is to be there for yourself, a daily act of presence that builds a foundation of self-love, as steady as a heartbeat.

This is soul alchemy. You are transforming the way you see yourself, literally and energetically. The mirror becomes more than glass; it becomes a portal to truth. At first, it might sting. But over time, as you show up, your reflection begins to smile back not with criticism, but with recognition.

You are not your scars. You are the one who survived them. And when tended to properly, even scars can fade.

Journaling: The Sacred Script of the Soul

And then there's journaling, a sacred conversation with your deepest self, where your thoughts flow like a river, uncovering truths you didn't know you held. In medieval monasteries, scribes wrote to commune with the soul, their words a bridge to clarity.

Journaling as a dialogue invites you to ask, "What am I holding back?" or "What does my heart need to say?" Each evening, you might sit with a notebook, letting your pen move without censor, writing as if your inner child or shadow is speaking.

You could ask your younger self, "What hurt you today?" or your shadow, "What are you afraid to show?" and let their answers spill onto the page. This practice, done with patience, becomes a mirror for your unconscious, revealing fears, dreams, and quiet strengths.

You might write, "I'm sorry you felt unseen," to your inner child, or "I see your anger, and it's okay," to your shadow, letting each word be a step toward wholeness.

And don't worry if the words don't come out poetic or clear. This isn't for performance. This is for liberation. The pen is your permission slip to feel, to unravel, to reclaim.

Let your journal be your witness, your healer, your mapmaker.

The Dance of Return: You Are the Sanctuary

These practices, holding your inner child, embracing your shadow, meeting your mirror, writing your soul's song, are not separate paths but a single dance, a gentle rebellion against the lies that trauma taught you. They ask you to move slowly, to trust that healing is a spiral, and to circle back with new tenderness.

Carl Jung saw the self as a whole that emerges when we integrate light and shadow, a process of becoming that honors every part of you.

These practices create a refuge within, a place where nothing needs to be hidden or managed to be allowed. What you once pushed away is no longer something to conquer or suppress, but something you can stand beside without fear.

Rainer Maria Rilke, poet and philosopher, once reflected that what frightens us often asks to be met with courage and attention. Not to be defeated, but to be understood. What lives beneath the surface of you isn't an enemy. It's unfinished communication. It's history asking for perspective. It's truth waiting to be met without distortion.

Your hidden self is not a flaw. It's a reserve of insight, strength, and self-knowledge that has been waiting for your readiness. Each time you listen instead of react, stay present instead of shutting down, or meet yourself honestly instead of harshly, you reclaim ground that once felt unsafe.

This is how you rebuild trust with yourself.
This is how wholeness takes shape.

You are not doing this work to become someone new. You are clearing the way to live as yourself, without fracture, without apology, without fear of what you'll find when you look inward.

- Step one, awareness.
- Step two, accountability.
- Step three, determination to regain control.

Move forward with steadiness.
You are already capable of holding what arises.
And you no longer need to run from your own depth.

CHAPTER 5

The Death of Who I Was – Ego, Archetypes, and Rebirth

Let us pause for a moment.

Before we move into this next chapter, I invite you to take a sacred breath; a moment of reflection to honor the journey you've already walked. The inner child work, the shadow work, and the raw honesty of journaling weren't just warm-ups, they were sacred initiations. Each of those actions asked you to meet yourself, layer by layer, in the dark. To listen to the voices you silenced. To hold the pieces of you that were once too messy, too needy, too painful to look at.

Why? Because you can't shed a self you haven't yet fully met. You can't release an identity if you've never examined the parts of you that created it. That's why the work had to begin there.

Now, with those roots unearthed, we're ready.
This is the death before the rebirth.
This is where we crawl into the chrysalis, where the old self dissolves into something unrecognizable, sacred, and alive.

This is the "goo" phase, the part most people don't talk about. Inside the chrysalis, the caterpillar doesn't grow wings and fly. It melts into a formless, cellular soup. Everything it was breaks down. And only from that total undoing can the butterfly take shape.

This is that moment.
The undoing.
The beginning of becoming.
This is where the ego dies so your true life can finally begin.

What Is Ego Death, Really?

Ego death is not the destruction of self, but the crumbling of illusion. It is the moment when your false identities (crafted from wounds, survival instincts, roles, and cultural conditioning) can no longer hold. It's not a fire that consumes indiscriminately. It's a sacred burn; a cleansing, a psychic wildfire meant to clear the way for your most authentic self.

Most of us live with an ego that has been layered over time, like sediment in a riverbed. There's the achiever, the pleaser, the rebel, the good girl, the provider, and the one who never asks for help. These personas are clever adaptations, built to keep us safe in a world that didn't always honor our sensitivity or truth.

But the thing about safety mechanisms is that they weren't designed for expansion. The ego, while essential in helping us navigate society, was never meant to be the pilot of the soul.

Ego death is the moment when we realize our mask has begun to suffocate us. It is the breakdown before the breakthrough. It is the invitation to stop performing and start existing, to shed the skin that no longer fits. And, like any death, it is both terrifying and holy.

As Carl Jung said: "There is no coming to consciousness without pain."

But there is also no true freedom without shedding what is not you.

This is the point where the self begins to awaken beneath the scaffolding. This is where your healing becomes not just repair, but *redefinition.*

As Carl Jung wrote:"Until you make the unconscious conscious, it will direct your life and you will call it fate."

This is the moment of making the unconscious conscious.

Jung, Archetypes, and the Path to Wholeness

Carl Jung didn't just dabble in shadow and dream work, he mapped the terrain of the psyche like a cartographer of the soul. He believed that every human being's destiny is to become whole, not perfect. And the path to wholeness? It's through the unconscious. Through the very parts of ourselves we were taught to reject, deny, or hide.

At the heart of Jungian psychology is the concept of *individuation*, a lifelong process of integrating all parts of the self into a cohesive, aware, empowered whole. This isn't about becoming someone new. It's about remembering who you truly are beneath the masks and projections.

Jung's archetypes help us decode these layers:

- The Persona: Our social mask, the role we play to be accepted.
- The Shadow: Our repressed, denied aspects, often holding both pain and power.
- The Anima/Animus: Our inner feminine/masculine energies that need balancing.
- The Self: The whole, divine essence of who we are, the bridge between psyche and soul.

When ego death begins, it's often the collapse of the Persona. We can no longer pretend. We can no longer uphold a version of ourselves that was only ever meant to be temporary. And so, we begin a descent into the depths, often guided by dreams, breakdowns, grief, or synchronicities that call us home to the truth.

Jung writes, "One does not become enlightened by imagining figures of light, but by making the darkness conscious."

And that's the work. Not to escape into bliss, but to integrate the beast and the beauty. The rage and the reverence. The fear and the freedom.

This is the sacred journey into wholeness. This is the psychological version of a spiritual awakening.

Ego death is the collapse of the persona, the curated version of "you" that was built to be loved, admired, accepted, or protected. It often happens after:

- A deep trauma or awakening
- Shadow work or psychedelic therapy
- Massive life shifts (divorce, grief, spiritual crisis)

"The privilege of a lifetime is to become who you truly are."
— Carl Jung

What Ego Death Feels Like

Imagine waking up one day and not recognizing the script that you've been living. Your job feels foreign. Your relationships feel surface-level. Your dreams no longer excite you, and the mirror reflects a version of you that feels... outdated.

That's ego death.

It's not dramatic or always visible from the outside. It often happens in quiet moments. A whisper that turns into a roar: "This isn't who I really am."

Ego death feels like:

- **Confusion:** A sense of disorientation. You may ask, "Who am I without this title, this role, this persona?"
- **Grief:** You're mourning a version of you that served a purpose, even if it was built on survival.
- **Emptiness:** A void. The in-between. You're no longer who you were, and not yet who you're becoming.
- **Liberation:** A lightness, once the layers begin to fall away. A sense of clarity rising in the stillness.

This is not a crisis. It's an awakening. But awakening isn't always blissful. It can be brutal. Like ripping a costume off skin it has fused to. Like realizing you've been holding your breath for years and only now learning how to inhale fully.

But beneath the ache is a truth: You are closer than ever to your essence.

The Neuroscience of Identity & Ego

Science and spirituality aren't at odds, they're just speaking different dialects of the same truth. Neuroscience offers powerful insight into what happens in the brain during ego death and identity collapse.

Much of our sense of self is governed by the Default Mode Network (DMN), a system in the brain responsible for self-referential thoughts, mental time travel (replaying the past or imagining the future), and the narrative we tell ourselves about who we are.

When the DMN is highly active, we tend to ruminate. We cling to identity. We rehearse pain. But studies show that during deep meditation, flow states, breathwork, and psychedelic experiences, the DMN quiets, and people experience:

- A loss of separation between self and other
- A sense of universal connection or spiritual oneness
- A release of deeply entrenched beliefs
- A profound increase in emotional insight and healing

What's happening here isn't just metaphor, it's biological. The brain relaxes its grip on identity. It stops running the "I am this, I am not that" program, and what emerges is often described as blissful, transcendent, or holy.

In trauma survivors, this process can feel like a reset. The rigid patterns of self-definition (often built to cope) soften, and in that softness, we find the freedom to rewrite the script.

This is why ego death is healing, even when it's disorienting. It rewires the brain. It interrupts the loop. It allows space for a new, healthier identity to be integrated from the inside out.

The Spiritual Perspective: The Dark Night of the Soul

Every mystic, saint, healer, and hero has walked through a "dark night." This night is the sacred unraveling that precedes becoming. In spiritual language, ego death is called the *dark night of the soul*; a phrase that sounds poetic but feels like hell.

This is not spiritual bypassing. It's not love and light. It's the part where everything you thought was true... isn't. Where God feels silent. Where the Universe goes quiet. Where your prayers return unanswered.

But in that silence, something deeper begins to stir. Because the dark night is not punishment. It's preparation.

During this stage, you are being emptied of what is false. Of what no longer fits. Of what cannot come with you into your next level of soul expansion.

You may:

- Lose relationships that were built on a version of you that no longer exists
- Feel depressed or untethered as your old joys fade
- Resist letting go, even as you know the ending is inevitable

And yet...

The dark night is a womb, not a grave. You are not dying, you are gestating. Everything you once were is dissolving into sacred soil. The compost of your next becoming.

Let yourself be held in the mystery. Let yourself grieve the old life. Let yourself melt before you fly.

You're not broken.

You're becoming the butterfly.

How to Navigate Ego Death

Ego death is not a single moment, it's a rite of passage. It doesn't knock politely and wait for your consent. It erupts when your soul is ready, whether your mind agrees or not. And when it arrives, it does not come with a manual.

There is grief. Grief for the identity you wore like armor. Grief for the illusions you lived inside. Grief for the self you thought would be enough, if only you worked harder, loved better, or fixed more.

But that grief is sacred. Because grieving the old self makes space for the real one.

Carl Jung observed that "the most terrifying thing is to accept oneself completely," highlighting how deep self-acceptance lies at the heart of true psychological maturity. Here in the ashes of your ego, you're asked to do just that. To meet yourself beyond labels, roles, performance, and projections. To hold the vastness of your becoming.

The first stage is disorientation. The mind scrambles to restore control. You may feel like you're floating in a fog, or like your past achievements and dreams no longer belong to you. This is normal. You are not lost. You're just between stories.

Then comes the silence. A void. A spiritual cocoon. You may feel disconnected from the world, uninterested in small talk, and repelled by anything that rings false. Let yourself go inward. Don't rush to rebuild.

Jung described the psychological task of withdrawing projections, recognizing and retrieving the parts of ourselves we have unconsciously placed onto others, as essential to becoming whole and conscious. We stop expecting the world to complete us. We begin reclaiming our own wholeness.

This is when your nervous system needs the most love. Breathe. Touch the earth. Eat grounding foods. Do less. Feel more. Ego death isn't a performance, it's a sacred surrender. Let the breakdown happen.

And then, something subtle shifts. A spark. A soft voice that whispers, "You are not gone. You are being rewritten."

You begin to notice beauty again. You begin to play with new desires. You sense that something wiser, deeper, and freer is waiting to take the lead.

That's the Self emerging. Not the small "s" self of habits and opinions, but the capital "S" Self that Jung described as the totality of the psyche. The part of you that existed before conditioning. Before fear. Before the mask.

This Self doesn't need validation to exist. It doesn't rush to fix or prove. It simply *is*.

When you lead from this place, your life reorganizes. You stop chasing, and start attracting. You stop performing, and start radiating. You stop gripping control, and start co-creating.

So if you're in the thick of it, if you're sobbing on your bathroom floor or staring at the ceiling wondering who the hell you are now, take heart. This is the holy unraveling. The spiritual compost. The chrysalis goo.

You are not dying. You are deepening.

Let the old self burn. Let the false idols fall. Let your soul take the wheel.

Because what comes next is the *you* that was always waiting to be born.

And you? You were always the phoenix.

A New Self Is Emerging

This is the spiritual surgery you didn't know you needed. It's raw. It's confusing. It's holy.

But it's clearing the path. For the truest version of you. For the life your soul actually signed up for. For the power, clarity, and freedom you couldn't access while clinging to the old skin.

This chapter ends not with a bow, but with an open door.

On the other side is *integration*. The daily becoming. The glow-up embodiment.

Next we will discuss how to walk in your new timeline without losing the softness of who you've become. How to integrate this soul shift and why integration is crucial.

Let's rise.

CHAPTER 6

Integration – Living the Awakening

You've walked through the fire. Faced the shadow. Sat with your inner child. You've released identities, dismantled illusions, and stood naked in the aftermath of ego death.

Now what?

Now, you integrate.

If ego death is the crumbling of who you were, integration is the sacred reconstruction. It's the art of living as your new self, without defaulting to the old programming. Integration is where insight becomes embodiment. Where healing becomes lifestyle. Where awakening stops being a concept and starts becoming a conversation between your soul and your every breath.

Carl Jung spoke of this process as *individuation*: the ongoing, conscious integration of all aspects of the psyche into wholeness. He didn't say the goal was to transcend the human self, but to live as a complete one. To be both divine and grounded. To marry the shadow with the light. Integration, in this way, is not an afterthought; it is the work.

> *"You are not meant to become perfect. You are meant to become whole."* —Carl Jung

So, what exactly is Integration?

Integration isn't just a buzzword or a spiritual catchphrase. It's the sacred and often uncomfortable bridge between insight and embodiment. It's waking up the morning after a life-altering realization and asking, "Now how do I live with this truth?"

To integrate is to take your revelations, those moments of clarity that cracked you open, and begin folding them into your reality. It's the deliberate, conscious process of creating a life that matches your frequency. That means aligning your job, your relationships, your food, your rest, your conversations, your nervous system, and your boundaries with the truth of who you are becoming.

It's not easy. You will be tested. Life will hand you mirrors. The world will invite you to return to your old roles, your old reactivity, your old masks. But now you know better. And when you know better, the universe nudges you, sometimes gently, sometimes loudly, to live better.

Integration is not the glamorous part of the journey. It's the gritty, sometimes awkward rehearsal of your new identity. It's where the spiritual meets the mundane. Where "I am worthy," becomes "I no longer answer that text." Where "I love myself," becomes "I went to bed early, drank water, and set a boundary."

This is where your power lives now.

Why Integration Matters

Healing without integration becomes spiritual bypassing. It's like learning the theory of flight but refusing to leave the runway. The insight alone feels good, enlightening, even. But without rooted action, it becomes a loop of awakening without embodiment.

When you fail to integrate, you feel stuck. Like you've read the manual but still can't build the machine. Your nervous system doesn't catch up. Your mind races ahead, but your body still flinches when triggered. Your soul screams expansion, but your habits pull you backward. This dissonance creates pain, and often, unnecessary suffering.

But when you *do* integrate? Magic.

The same trigger that once collapsed you now becomes a portal into presence. The same relationship that once drained you is now released with compassion. The same fear that kept you small becomes a lighthouse for transformation.

Integration rewires your body to match your beliefs. It calibrates your subconscious. It makes healing sustainable. Without it, you risk awakening only to fall back asleep. With it, you rise - not as a different person, but as your real one.

Integration is where the healing *sticks*. It's how your nervous system finds safety in expansion. It's where your soul starts to feel at home in your body again.

This is where you start to remember you're not just healing. You're rebuilding a foundation that can actually hold joy.

From Insight to Identity

There's a quiet revolution that happens when you stop outsourcing your worth and start building a life that reflects your internal shift. That's the power of integration: it transforms fleeting inspiration into long-term identity.

It's in the pause before you respond to an old trigger. It's in the softness with which you greet yourself in the mirror. It's in the way you choose presence over performance.

Each conscious decision is a brick laid in the architecture of your new self.

You are no longer reacting from the blueprint of survival. You are creating from the blueprint of consciousness.

That means you'll start designing a life based on what nurtures your nervous system, what aligns with your boundaries, and what honors your essence, not what others expect.

Carl Jung would call this the "journey toward the Self," a transcendent yet grounded state of unity within the psyche. It's where the persona dissolves and the essence begins to speak louder than the ego ever did.

So when you ask:

- "How does the healed version of me move through the world?"
- "What feels expansive, not performative?"

- "What would I choose if I truly trusted myself?"

You're not just reflecting. You're *rebuilding*. And the answers to these questions don't just shift your days, they reshape your destiny.

Jung and the Mandala of Wholeness

To Jung, the mandala represented more than art. It was a map of the soul, a cosmic diagram of the Self in balance. When you integrate, you are literally drawing your own mandala, one conscious choice at a time. Each act becomes a self-reclamation of colors in a new section.

Wholeness, in Jungian terms, is not about perfection. It's about integration. It's about reclaiming the banished pieces: the wild, the messy, the sensual, the angry, the soft.

It's about saying, "All of me gets to exist here."

In a culture obsessed with perfection and performance, this is radical.

When you embrace the full spectrum of who you are, you shift from fragmentation to fullness. You stop trying to be palatable and start becoming powerful. You don't just create balance, you become it.

You become the still point in the storm. The eye of your own awakening.

This is what your integration gives birth to: self who can hold paradoxes. Who can cry and still be strong. Who can grieve and still be joyful. Who can shatter and still shine.

You don't exile any part of you anymore.

They're all invited and they all have wisdom.

The Daily Practice of Integration

This is the part that no one claps for. No one hands you a certificate when you drink water instead of wine. No one throws a parade when you meditate instead of dissociate. But *this* is where the transformation becomes a way of life.

Daily integration is not about being perfect. It's about being present.

Every time that you choose rest over burnout, you're integrating. Every time that you speak your truth without shrinking, you're integrating. Every time that you pause instead of react, you're integrating.

Daily integration is about casting votes for the life you want with each micro-moment.

The real transformation doesn't happen in one big psychedelic breakthrough. It happens in the way you choose to live each and every day. In the way that you breathe through the next wave of anxiety. In the way that you answer the next text from someone who once had power over you.

This is the invisible miracle of *becoming*.

Let your rituals be your resistance. Let your boundaries be your healing. Let your joy be your activism.

Integration Is Not Linear

Expect it to be messy. It's not a clean arc, it's a spiral. Throughout the process, you will circle back to the same themes, but each time with more awareness, more strength, more softness. Be gentle with yourself.

One day, you'll feel like a mystic in alignment with every atom in the cosmos. The next day, you'll forget everything and cry on your kitchen floor. This is integration.

You are a wave. Let yourself ebb and flow.

Jung reminded us that, *"we don't become enlightened by imagining figures of light, but by making the darkness conscious."* This includes the darkness of self-judgment when you relapse into old habits. The key is not to punish yourself, but to return.

Integration is not a destination. It's a devotion. A homecoming, again and again.

What Happens Next?

You've dismantled. You've excavated. You've cracked open. And now?

Now you rebuild.

From here, we begin embodiment. Not just energetically, but physiologically. We'll explore how meditation, frequency, nervous system regulation, and conscious energy work create a life where you're not just surviving, but radiating through.

We are not going back. We are going *inward*, then *upward*.

Because this time, you're not doing it from a wound. You're doing it from wisdom.

You've broken open. Let's build.

CHAPTER 7

Where Energy Flows, Life Grows

Picture yourself on a beach at midnight. The waves are whispering secrets sharp enough to slice through your doubts. The stars aren't twinkling, they're blazing with truths that outshine the world's greatest performers. The universe is listening and, more importantly, you are too.

Because this is where it gets electric.

Welcome to the art of energy; your soul's radiant current, the invisible thread that weaves your thoughts, breath, and spirit into a force powerful enough to light cities, bend timelines, and heal legacies.

When your energy is blocked, it's like a symphony that is stuck on mute. But when it flows? You're conducting a masterpiece, vibrating so fiercely the world can't help but hum along.

This chapter is your guide to unleashing that current through meditation, chakra alignment, forgiveness, and high-frequency living.

As we say at The Glow Up Project, "Your energy isn't just a vibe, it's the pulse that reshapes your world."

Energy Isn't Woo, It's Physics With a Pulse

Energy is your essence. It's the buzz that lives in your veins, your laugh when no one's watching, the shiver up your spine when truth hits home. It's not just some mystical concept, it's the physics of your existence.

Your thoughts spark electricity in your neurons. Your heart emits a measurable electromagnetic field. Your emotions broadcast frequencies. In short: you are a walking, humming orchestra of vibration.

Block that flow, and life feels heavy, disconnected, mechanical. Let it move, and suddenly your cells, your spirit, and your reality begin to shift.

Fear knots your energy. Joy sets it soaring.

Shame dims your light. Forgiveness turns it golden.

Modern science is catching up to what Vedic sages, Taoist mystics, and Indigenous healers knew millennia ago: Energy is life's currency, and *you are the boss of your own reserves.*

Emotions like gratitude and compassion bring the brain and heart into a state of coherence, making your energy magnetic. Henri Bergson, with his philosophy of vital energy, saw life as a surge of creative force that flows when we align with truth. Your pain, your passion, your purpose? All made of the same thing: *energy, waiting to be directed.*

Meditation: Reclaiming the Airwaves

Meditation is a reclamation of your inner world. It's how you pause the noise, tune into your breath, and reconnect with the clearest, wisest part of you.

In just a few quiet minutes, you shift from reactivity to presence. You reset your nervous system. You lower stress hormones. You strengthen the parts of your brain responsible for clarity, compassion, and emotional resilience.

Think of it as sitting in your internal command center, where you choose your energy, your focus, your truth.

For thousands of years, mystics, monks, and seekers have used stillness to align with something deeper: the pulse of the earth, the rhythm of the stars, the frequency of healing. That same power is available to you, right now, right here, no incense or mountain top required.

Close your eyes. Breathe deep. Go inward.

The Brainwave Symphony

Your brain is a living radio station, constantly broadcasting different "stations" of consciousness. These stations are brainwave frequencies, electrical patterns created by your neurons as they fire. Meditation isn't about turning the radio off, it's about changing the channel to the one that heals, restores, and awakens.

The Art & Science of Frequency-Understanding Brainwaves and Human Potential

What Are Brainwaves?

Your brain is a bioelectrical field. Neurons communicate via tiny electrical impulses that produce brainwaves, measured in hertz (Hz), cycles per second. These brainwaves are *not just mental activity*, they influence your nervous system, hormones, mood, cognition, spiritual experiences, and your ability to manifest, heal, or collapse timelines.

There are five core brainwave states (with some subdivisions), each with unique properties:

Frequency Band	Hz Range	State Associated With
Gamma	30–100 Hz	Peak awareness, unity consciousness, bliss
Beta	12–30 Hz	Normal waking, focus, stress, thinking
Alpha	8–12 Hz	Calm, relaxed, meditative
Theta	4–8 Hz	Deep meditation, hypnosis, subconscious
Delta	0.5–4 Hz	Deep sleep, regeneration, unconscious

Why Higher Frequencies (Like Gamma) Relate to Enlightenment

At first glance, it seems paradoxical: The deeper you go into the subconscious, the slower your brainwaves... yet enlightenment is the fastest one?

Here's how it makes sense:

- **Gamma (30–100 Hz)** is the only frequency found across the *entire brain at once*. It's associated with peak awareness, spiritual ecstasy, compassion, love, and deep insight.

- Tibetan monks and advanced meditators have extreme levels of gamma, even at rest. Gamma represents an *integrated state* (all parts of the brain firing in unison). It's not chaos, it's coherence.
- Enlightenment isn't just about going "deeper" into stillness. It's about going deeper *and* higher, simultaneously:
  - Gamma = Unity consciousness
  - Theta = Subconscious rewiring
  - Delta = Divine cellular repair

You are meant to surf across all of them.

Gamma happens when you're not "trying" to achieve anything, but simply *being*.

The Frequencies of Love, Compassion & Manifestation

While brainwaves are one lens, emotions also have frequencies, a concept validated by researchers like Dr. David Hawkins (author of *Power vs. Force*), who mapped human emotions on a vibrational frequency scale. The frequency values below are symbolic rather than neurological measurements, reflecting a metaphorical framework often used in contemplative traditions rather than EEG-based neuroscience.

Emotion	Frequency (Hz)	Brainwave Ranges Often Linked
Enlightenment	700–900	Gamma
Peace	600	Gamma
Love	500	Alpha/Gamma
Joy	540	Alpha/Theta
Compassion	500+	Gamma
Courage	200	High Beta/Alpha
Shame	20	Low Beta/Theta
Guilt	30	Low Beta
Fear	100	Mid Beta

When you're in a state of love, compassion, and joy, your heart and brain begin to *entrain* to one another. This is called heart-brain coherence, and it's the biological foundation of:

- Intuition
- Flow states
- Manifestation
- Healing miracles

What Are We Aiming for Spiritually?

We're not trying to *live* in just one frequency.

We're aiming for fluid access across the spectrum, with longer states of:

- **Theta** for subconscious reprogramming (inner child, trauma healing)
- **Alpha/Gamma** for heart coherence and present-moment awareness
- **Gamma** for spiritual embodiment and unity consciousness
- **Delta** during sleep for divine cellular rejuvenation

Your *Higher Self* is not in one wave, it's in the harmony of all of them.

You're not here to "ascend" and escape the human.

You're here to bridge the cosmos and the cellular.

You are both antenna and receiver. Tuning fork and frequency.

How to Access Specific Frequencies

Goal	Target State	Tools & Practices
Trauma healing	Theta	Hypnosis, guided inner child meditations
Daily stress relief	Alpha	Breathwork, nature walks, soft music

Goal	Target State	Tools & Practices
Deep rest & body repair	Delta	Deep sleep, binaural beats
Spiritual expansion	Gamma	Open focus meditation, gratitude, love
Manifestation flow	Alpha/Theta	Visualization, future journaling, scripting
Creativity boost	Alpha	Journaling, painting, walking meditations

Brain entrainment tools like binaural beats, frequency-based music (e.g. 432 Hz), and meditation apps can help induce these states.

Final Truth: You Are a Frequency Generator

You are not just a body.
You are a field. A frequency. A living waveform.

When you feel "off," You are out of resonance.

Your job isn't to force healing, it's to retune yourself.
Your thoughts, environment, food, breath, and even people around you are influencing your state at all times.

Healing isn't about doing more.
It's about tuning into what's already whole inside you.

I once heard a quote that stuck with me, its origin unknown, but its truth undeniable:
"The day you stop trying to fix yourself and start feeling yourself... is the day you begin to heal."

That line lives in my bones. Because healing begins when you come home to yourself. When you allow your emotions to move, your truth to surface, and your body to speak. That's where the real transformation starts, in feeling fully, bravely, and without apology.

The Science of Soul Repair

Meditation changes the physical structure of your brain. Studies using MRI scans show that regular practice shrinks the amygdala (your brain's fear center) and thickens the prefrontal cortex (the part responsible for emotional regulation, decision-making, and empathy). It also directly stimulates your vagus nerve, the superhighway of your parasympathetic nervous system. This activation slows your heart rate, improves digestion, lowers inflammation, and shifts you into rest-and-digest mode.

How to Reclaim Your Airwaves

1. Find Your Anchor – Sit or lie down comfortably.
2. Breathe with Intention – Inhale for 4, hold for 4, exhale for 6.
3. Pick a Signal – A mantra, single word, or sound of your breath.
4. Expect Static – Mind wandering is normal. Redirect gently.
5. Stay 10 Minutes – Start with 3 if needed, increase over time.

Supercharging Your Meditation: The Science-Backed Power-Ups

Once you know the basics of brainwaves, you can hack your way into deeper states even faster. This is where ancient wisdom meets cutting-edge neuroscience.

Brainwave Entrainment – Borrowing the Frequency: Your brain matches steady rhythms, shifting into desired states faster. Includes binaural beats and isochronic tones.

Sound Therapy – Medicine You Can Hear: Certain frequencies stimulate healing. Examples: 432 Hz (love frequency), 528 Hz (miracle tone).

Visualization – The Mind's Reality Printer: The subconscious can't tell imagined from real, use sensory-rich mental imagery for healing.

Coherence Breathing – Syncing Heart & Mind: Inhale and exhale evenly, focusing on the heart. Promotes Alpha–Theta blend.

The Daily Dose: Micro-meditations of 2–3 minutes throughout the day shift your baseline brainwaves over time.

Meditation isn't a passive escape, it's an active reprogramming of your biology, your mind, and your energy field. Add sound, visualization, and breath, and you've got a spiritual operating system upgrade. You're not just sitting still. You're turning your brain into a broadcasting tower for peace, clarity, and possibility.

Chakras: Your Soul's Control Panel

These seven swirling energy centers from your spine to your crown aren't just pretty symbols on a yoga mat, they are your inner power grid. Each one governs specific aspects of your physical health, emotional well-being, and spiritual connection. When one goes offline, the system glitches. But when they're aligned? Everything flows. You're lit from the inside out.

A Little History Lesson

The word 'chakra' comes from Sanskrit, meaning 'wheel' or 'disk.' First referenced in ancient Vedic texts thousands of years ago, chakras were described as spinning vortexes of energy; bridges between the physical body and the subtle (energetic) body.

Over centuries, chakra knowledge traveled through India, Tibet, China, and into Western esoteric traditions. Yogis mapped them through meditation and breathwork, Chinese medicine addressed similar energy points through meridians, and Indigenous cultures had their own systems of energy centers. No matter the name or culture, the message was the same: energy flows where attention goes.

The Science Behind the Spin

Each chakra corresponds to a nerve plexus (bundle of nerves) and endocrine gland:

- Root Chakra: Pelvic plexus and adrenal glands.
- Sacral Chakra: Reproductive glands.

- Solar Plexus Chakra: Pancreas.
- Heart Chakra: Thymus gland.
- Throat Chakra: Thyroid gland.
- Third Eye Chakra: Pituitary gland.
- Crown Chakra: Pineal gland.

When you focus awareness on a chakra, you stimulate the nervous system, influence hormone release, and shift brainwave patterns. Aligning chakras can boost mood, immunity, and intuition.

The Seven Chakras – Glow-Up Style

Root (Red) – Foundation, safety, survival. When blocked: anxiety, instability.

> Glow-Up Move: visualize roots, walk barefoot. Affirm: 'I am safe. I belong here.'

Sacral (Orange) – Sensuality, creativity, emotions. When blocked: low libido, guilt.

> Glow-Up Move: dance, hip stretches, water immersion. Affirm: 'I am free to feel.'

Solar Plexus (Yellow) – Confidence, willpower, personal power. When blocked: self-doubt, procrastination.

> Glow-Up Move: core exercises, laughter, sun exposure. Affirm: 'I am powerful.'

Heart (Green) – Love, compassion, emotional balance. When blocked: grief, guardedness.

> Glow-Up Move: heart-opening yoga, gratitude journaling. Affirm: 'My heart is open and free.'

Throat (Blue) – Communication, truth, self-expression. When blocked: fear of speaking, dishonesty.

> Glow-Up Move: singing, affirmations aloud. Affirm: 'I speak with clarity and courage.'

Third Eye (Indigo) – Intuition, clarity, higher perspective. When blocked: indecision, overthinking.

> Glow-Up Move: meditation, dream journaling. Affirm: 'I trust my inner knowing.'

Crown (Violet/White) – Spiritual connection, divine guidance. When blocked: feeling lost, disconnected.

> Glow-Up Move: prayer, stargazing, silence. Affirm: 'I am guided.'

Balancing the Grid

Ancient cultures used acupuncture, sound healing, crystal therapy, and movement practices like qigong to reset these energy centers.

Today, you can use:

- Sound: Chanting each chakra's seed syllable (LAM, VAM, RAM, YAM, HAM, OM, silence).
- Visualization: Imagining each chakra as a spinning ball of its color.
- Touch: Placing your hand over a chakra with intention.
- Movement: Yoga poses, dance, or stretches for the chakra's body area.

You don't need a guru or certification to be sovereign in your own energy. You are the keeper of your grid.

The Science of Alignment

Balancing your chakras aligns your autonomic nervous system, reduces stress hormones, and increases coherence between your heart and brain. It can also boost neuroplasticity, which is your brain's ability to rewire itself. After chakra work, people often feel lighter, calmer, and more focused.

Your Glow-Up Challenge

Today, pick one chakra you feel is off and spend five minutes focusing on it:

- Visualize it spinning freely.
- Breathe in its color.
- Speak its affirmation.
- Move the part of your body it governs.

Energy moves where you put your awareness. When you take control of your soul's control panel, you take control of your life.

Forgiveness – The Ultimate Frequency Upgrade

Ah, forgiveness. The big one. The energy reboot that no one wants to do, but everyone needs. And no, forgiveness is not about condoning toxic behavior, playing doormat, or pretending it didn't hurt. It's not about a Hallmark card moment or an overnight miracle.

Forgiveness is a spiritual power move.

Forgiveness is about cutting the cord between your power and their behavior. It's an energy detox. An emotional decluttering. A deep spiritual shower after swimming in someone else's poison for too long.

This is not about sending love and roses to the one who broke you, it's about calling your energy back from where it's been leaking.

It's standing in the rubble and saying, *"You don't get to live here anymore."*

The Science of Letting Go

Your brain stores resentment like a bad file that you keep opening. Each time you replay the hurt, your amygdala (the brain's fear and threat center) lights up. Cortisol floods your body. Your heart rate spikes. Your immune system drops. Your nervous system doesn't know the difference between the original wound and the replay. It thinks it's happening again.

Chronic unforgiveness traps you in fight-or-flight mode. Over time, this can lead to anxiety, depression, insomnia, digestive issues, and inflammation. It's not just emotional baggage, it's biological stress that prematurely ages your cells.

Forgiveness isn't letting someone "win." It's switching off the alarm that's been blaring in your body for years. It's reclaiming mental bandwidth. It's lowering your stress hormones so your immune system can actually do its job.

The Spiritual Physics of Forgiveness

Energy follows focus. When you hold onto anger, you are energetically tethered to the very thing you want to escape. This is why some people keep living rent-free in your head long after they're gone.

Forgiveness severs that tether. It collapses the energetic bridge that keeps your life force tied to their actions. It doesn't erase what happened, it releases your soul from the loop.

Think of it like upgrading your frequency. Resentment vibrates heavy and low. Forgiveness moves you up the scale, closer to love, compassion, and peace, not because they deserve it, but because *you do*.

It's Not Always About You

Most of the time, the hurt that someone causes you has little to do with you at all. Their betrayal, their cruelty, and their withdrawal often stems from their own unhealed wounds, buried shame, and unresolved trauma. Their behavior is a mirror reflecting *their* pain, not your worth.

You weren't too much. You weren't not enough. They just couldn't meet you where you were because they hadn't yet met themselves.

This doesn't justify harm, but it helps you step out of self-blame and into clarity. And if you truly feel you've shown up in your integrity (done your work, communicated with compassion, healed your own patterns) then don't keep picking up the guilt they dropped at your feet.

Forgiveness becomes the act of compassionately releasing the story that their behavior meant something was wrong with you. It's energetic sovereignty. You don't need to live in the guilt of leaving somebody who refuses to heal. It is not your job to heal them or to carry their burdens forever. You can find peace in standing in your truth, that you deserve better, you deserve someone willing to put in the work. You can still love someone, even if you must do it from afar. Sometimes, walking away, standing in your truth and letting them sit with theirs, is the most powerful act of love you could perform...to them, and to yourself.

Compassion Without Justification

This is not a hall pass for toxic behavior. It's not a green light to avoid your own reflection. Because sometimes, the truth is: *you* played a role, too.

Self-reflection is a non-negotiable in healing. You must ask:

- Am I reacting from my own trauma?
- Is there a pattern I keep replaying?
- What in me attracted or tolerated this dynamic?

And if you find the truth there, own it. That's where your power lives.

But here's the line: If someone outright hurts you, blames you for everything, can't meet your needs, or manipulates you into shrinking, that's not on you.

I learned this the hard way in my marriage to a narcissist. It took years to untangle myself from the emotional whiplash, to realize that his blame and gaslighting weren't signs that I was broken, but that *he* was. I don't accept his behavior. But I no longer own it. I no longer let it

poison my nervous system. I've made peace with his pain, because
that's the only way I could reclaim mine.

How to Forgive Without Faking It

- **Name the Hurt** – Say what happened and how it impacted you. This is truth-telling, not weakness.
- **Separate the Person from the Pattern** – See the wound in them without excusing the wound they gave you.
- **Call Your Energy Back** – Visualize a cord, stretching from your chest to theirs, dissolving. See your energy returning.
- **Release in Writing** – Write a letter you'll never send. End with: *"I see your wound, but I release mine."*
- **Fill the Space** – Replace the void with breathwork, prayer, nature, or music.

Forgiveness ≠ Reconciliation

Forgiving doesn't mean forgetting, trusting again, or reuniting. You can forgive and still maintain a no-contact policy. You can release the weight without re-entering the fire.

Forgiveness is a radical act of self-liberation, it is strength in motion, one of the bravest ways to take your power back. It's taking the driver's seat in your own nervous system and saying, *"I choose peace over poison."*

The Glow-Up Challenge: 7-Day Forgiveness Ritual

Day 1 – Name the person or event.
Day 2 – Write the story exactly as your heart feels it.
Day 3 – Identify how it's still impacting your life today.
Day 4 – Write what you learned about yourself because of it.
Day 5 – Visualize calling your energy back.
Day 6 – Speak the release aloud: *"I free myself from this story."*
Day 7 – Replace the space with something joyful or sacred.

Forgiveness is not about making peace with them. It's about making peace with *you*. It's not about the past, it's about clearing your frequency so your future has room to grow.

When you forgive, you are not letting them off the hook. You are simply unhooking yourself.

High-Frequency Living: Your Daily Soul Rituals

Let's be real, life can be heavy. The world can be loud. And energy leaks are real.

That's where high-frequency living becomes your spiritual hygiene, a rhythm shaped not by perfectionism but by mindful engagement. It begins with the quiet, repeated choices that recalibrate your energy.

- Gratitude every morning, three things.
- Move your body. Dance like no one's judging.
- Be in nature. Touch a tree. Let the Earth recalibrate you.
- Laugh. Loudly. Even if it's at memes.
- Cut the energy vampires loose.
- Use music that lifts you, not just trendy, but vibrationally aligned.
- Drink water like it's a love letter to your cells.

This isn't fluff. This is science. Positive emotions stimulate your parasympathetic nervous system, reduce inflammation, and raise your electromagnetic field.

Translation? You become a walking beacon.

Your Vibe Shapes the Collective

I'll talk a lot about vibes throughout the book because it is the resounding message I want to convey. Your energy is contagious, a signal that echoes into the room, the world, the *collective field*.

Quantum physics tells us that everything is connected. Your vibration doesn't stop at your skin. It radiates. When you clear your energy, you shift your environment. When you rise, others feel it.

Meditate in the morning. Tap your heart chakra at noon. Forgive something old at night. Speak gratitude aloud before bed. These aren't just tasks, they are transmissions, and they create momentum that builds miracles.

When you align your energy, the Universe doesn't just notice, it *responds*.

Final Word: You Are Already Electric

Your energy is your power, a pulse that can light up the darkest corners, inside and out.

Every breath you take in stillness.
Every knot you untangle in meditation.
Every grudge you finally release.
Every high-frequency choice you make.
You are raising your vibration.
You are rewriting your story.
You are reclaiming your soul's signal.

You are not here to be muted. You are here to glow so brightly the darkness has no choice but to adjust.

As The Glow Up Project whispers: "Your energy isn't just a vibe, it's the pulse that reshapes your world."

Step into this flow.

You're already electric.

CHAPTER 8

Becoming the Alchemist – Embodying Your Shift

Picture yourself standing before a glowing crucible, its molten light dancing with the promise of transformation. Each spark is a whisper of the radiant self you're destined to become. The air hums with possibility, thick, potent, sharp, ready to transmute the raw ore of your past into pure gold.

They say it takes pressure to make diamonds, and I've said it too, more times than I can count. When people ask how I've endured what I've faced, how I keep moving through the fire, I come back to that truth. Because even in the heaviest moments, something in me refused to break. Something in me knew: this was the making.

That same knowing lives in you.

Welcome to the heart of *The Glow Up Project*, where you don't just change, you alchemize.
Where you don't just tweak habits, you forge a new reality.

This chapter is not a patch or a fix.
It is fire. It is elemental. It is Holy

You are no longer the seeker.
You are the alchemist.

You are not here to chase healing.
You are here to become the force that redefines what healing means.

This isn't about making peace with the past.
It's about gathering its fragments, throwing them into the crucible, and forging something sacred out of the burn.

Alchemy, once whispered by mystics in Egyptian temples and etched in the glyphs of Hermes Trismegistus, was never just about turning lead into gold. It was about turning suffering into sovereignty, fear into clarity, and the self into soul.

As Heraclitus wrote, "Change is the only constant; the fire within shapes all."

This chapter is your invitation to stoke that inner fire, fiercely, playfully, spiritually, and transmute everything.

Your pain is the ore.
Your heart is the forge.
Your life? A living spell.

You Are Both Scientist and Sorcerer

Your life is a laboratory, and you are both the curious observer and the divine conductor.

Your brain, that miraculous shapeshifter, holds a secret most of us were never taught: neuroplasticity, its ability to rewire itself in response to thought, intention, and experience.

This means that every single time you catch a self-sabotaging loop and choose something kinder, stronger, wiser, you are physically altering the architecture of your mind.

That's not poetic fluff, it's measurable on a brain scan. You are changing your mind, by changing your mind.

The Science of Shapeshifting

For centuries, scientists believed the adult brain was fixed, that your wiring was set in stone by your twenties. But advances in neuroscience have blown that myth apart. The brain is more like a living garden than a static machine. Every thought, every emotion, and every repeated behavior is either planting new seeds or feeding old weeds.

Here's what's happening under the hood when you "shift":

- **Synaptic Connections:** Neurons that fire together wire together. The more you repeat a thought or action, the stronger that neural pathway becomes.

- **Synaptic Pruning:** Just as unused trails grow over, neural connections you stop using will fade. When you stop feeding the circuit for self-doubt, it begins to wither.
- **Neurogenesis:** In certain brain regions (like the hippocampus), you can grow entirely new neurons, meaning new memory patterns, new emotional responses, and new creative abilities.

This is why intentional practices like meditation, visualization, affirmations, breathwork, and gratitude journaling aren't "woo-woo extras." They are biological reprogramming tools.

Spirit Meets Science

Science can measure the *how* of transformation, but Spirit holds the *why*.

Neuroplasticity is your body's mechanical blueprint for change; your soul is the architect.

When you visualize your highest self, you are not just playing pretend, you are sending electrical signals through your nervous system and emotional signatures through your energy field. These signals train your brain and inform your subconscious what to expect as "normal."

Many psychologists and educators often suggest that as much as 90–95% of mental processing occurs outside conscious awareness, reflecting the dominant role of automatic and nonconscious cognition. A rough estimate reflecting how much of our behavior is driven by habit, instinct, and automatic responses rather than deliberate thought. Your subconscious doesn't care if your input is positive or negative, she just runs the code you give her.

That's why blending neuroscience with spiritual intention is the ultimate power move: Science builds the pathway, spirit fuels the journey.

Rewiring in Real Time

Let's take an old, corrosive thought: *"I'm not enough."*

Here's the alchemy:

- **Catch it** – Awareness is the first key. Without it, you're running old code on autopilot.
- **Pause** – A breath interrupts the pattern and engages the prefrontal cortex (the part of your brain responsible for conscious choice).
- **Smirk** – Humor disarms the amygdala's stress response. You can't feel fear and genuine amusement at the same time.
- **Replace it** – "I am everything I need to be."
  Say it like you mean it. Feel it land in your body. Imagine it *glowing* in your cells.
- **Reinforce it** – Repeat daily, in writing, out loud, and in visualization until it feels second nature.

Do this consistently, and the shame circuit begins to dim. In its place? A blazing new trail toward self-worth.

The Daily Spell for Becoming

Try this:

- **Every Morning** – Sit for five minutes, eyes closed. Picture yourself, not as you were, not even as you are, but as your highest, most magnetic, unapologetically whole self. See it in detail: your posture, your voice, your smile, your environment, the energy you radiate.
- **Feel it** – Let your body register the sensation of already being that version of you. This is crucial, emotion is the chemical stamp that tells your brain, *This is real.*
- **Speak it** – A mantra, affirmation, or "I am" statement that aligns with that vision.
- **At Night** – Write it down in the present tense as if it's already true. This is your daily spell.

You're not hoping. You're programming.
You're not fantasizing. You're forging.

When Doubt Creeps In

It will. Doubt is just the echo of old wiring trying to survive. When it knocks, greet it like an uninvited salesman at your door:

- Smile.
- Shake your head.
- Say, "Not today, mind. I'm busy becoming art."

The Physics of Becoming the Shift

When you practice new thoughts and behaviors, your brain begins to:

- Fire more coherent brainwaves (less noise, more clarity).
- Synchronize your heart-brain connection, calming the nervous system.
- Release dopamine and serotonin as you visualize and embody joy.
- Activate mirror neurons, your body begins to "practice" the movements, expressions, and tone of your future self.

You literally start to become the person you've been rehearsing in your mind.

The Golden Truth

Neuroplasticity is the bridge.
Spirit is the current.
You are the architect.

Every thought you choose is either an incantation for your future or a chain to your past.
Choose wisely.

Because when you realize you are both scientist and sorcerer, you stop waiting for the world to shift, and you become the shift.

Boundaries: The Gates to Your Energy Kingdom

Boundaries aren't walls to keep the world out. They're gates to protect what's sacred. They are the architecture of your energy field, the invisible framework that keeps your soul from being siphoned, your heart from being trampled, and your time from being drained by chaos you never asked for.

When you set a boundary, you're not being "mean," "selfish," or "hard to deal with." You're honoring the truth of who you are. You're telling the universe, *This is the standard here.* And just like any healthy ecosystem, your internal world thrives when it's not being overrun by invasive weeds.

Why Boundaries Are Sacred

Your energy is currency.
Every conversation, task, favor, and interaction is either an investment or a withdrawal. Without boundaries, you'll keep giving overdraft after overdraft until your spirit is running on fumes.

Boundaries protect:

- Your energy – so you don't spend the day resentful and depleted.
- Your mental health – so you have space to think, feel, and create.
- Your relationships – because healthy limits breed respect, not resentment.
- Your alignment – so you're living according to your values, not someone else's script.

When you set and honor your boundaries, you're broadcasting to the universe, *I am worthy of peace, respect, and alignment.* The universe will match you with people, opportunities, and experiences that fit that frequency.

Boundaries for Yourself

Not all boundaries are about other people, many are about you. These are your personal contracts: the lines you won't cross with yourself because you know they'll cost you your energy, integrity, or peace.

Examples:

- "I don't scroll social media before my morning routine."
- "I won't commit to more than two major projects at once."
- "I will pause before saying 'yes' to anything new."

Self-boundaries are the quiet promises that keep your life in balance when no one's watching.

Boundaries With Others

When setting boundaries with people, remember: it's not about control. You're not dictating their behavior, you're simply defining what you will and will not participate in.

Instead of:

"You can't talk to me like that."

Say:

"I don't stay in conversations where I'm being yelled at. I'll step away until we can talk respectfully."

Instead of:

"You can't keep dumping last-minute work on me."

Say:

"I need at least 24 hours' notice to take on new tasks. If that's not possible, I'll have to pass."

Be clear, direct, and rooted in your own standard, not a personal attack.

Empowered, Not Rude

Boundaries lose their power when they're laced with bitterness. You can be loving and unshakable at the same time. The secret is tone: firm, grounded, and free from the need to over-explain or convince.

Think of it like a velvet rope at an exclusive event: polite, warm smile, but still... *No one gets past the rope without an invitation.*

The more you practice, the less you'll need to justify. A simple, "That doesn't work for me," is a full sentence.

Energetic Implications

From an energetic perspective, every boundary you set is like placing a tuning fork in the ground,

it vibrates a message. People and opportunities that match your vibration will naturally gravitate toward you.

Those that don't? They'll drift away without you needing to chase them off.

If you keep letting energy-draining situations linger, you're teaching the universe that you're okay with low-frequency experiences. Boundaries are how you say, *I only accept what's aligned with my worth.*

How to Strengthen Your Boundaries

1. **Get Clear on Your Values** – You can't guard what you haven't defined. Know what matters to you most.
2. **Listen to Your Body** – Anxiety, irritation, or exhaustion are often signs a boundary has been crossed.
3. **Start Small** – Practice saying "no" to low-stakes requests before tackling the bigger ones.
4. **Stand by Your Word** – A boundary without follow-through is just a wish.
5. **Release the Guilt** – Saying "yes" to yourself will always mean saying "no" to something else.

Boundary Mantra

"My peace is not negotiable. My energy is not for auction. My life is lived in alignment with my highest truth."

Boundaries aren't about keeping love out, they're about making sure love, respect, and opportunity can *stay in*.
They are the gates to your kingdom. Guard them with grace, and your world will flourish.

Conscious Creation: Your Reality Is the Result of Repetition

Creation isn't random. It's vibrational precision.
Your thoughts aren't just fleeting clouds drifting through your head. They are tuning forks, broadcasting frequencies that pull people, opportunities, and patterns into resonance with you.

What you focus on expands due to:

- **Cognitive Bias** – Your brain selectively filters information to confirm your existing beliefs. If you think opportunities are everywhere, you'll spot them. If you think you're unlucky, you'll miss the open doors right in front of you.
- **Mirror Neurons** – Your brain automatically reflects the emotions, energy, and behavior of what you observe, meaning your inner state directly influences the way others respond to you.
- **Neuroplasticity** – Repetition hardwires thought patterns into your brain, literally shaping your perception and behavior until they become your autopilot reality.

This is not fluff, it's physics, biology, and intention working in the same direction.

The Law of Attraction, De-wooed and Demystified

The Law of Attraction says: Like attracts like.
Science says: Your thoughts shape your perception, which shapes your decisions, which shapes your reality.

They are the same truth in different languages.

When you repeatedly hold a thought or feeling, you condition your nervous system and subconscious to expect it. Your Reticular Activating System (RAS), the brain's filter, then prioritizes information that matches this expectation. Suddenly, "miracles" seem to appear everywhere, but they've been there all along. You simply tuned yourself to see them.

Your Daily Creation Blueprint

Imagine this:

1. Wake up.
2. Visualize your highest self, confident, connected, abundant. See the details: where you live, how you move, the conversations you have, the way people light up in your presence.
3. Feel it, not as wishful thinking, but as if it's already done. Anchor the emotion in your body.
4. Act in alignment with that frequency. Take one small action, make the call, sign up for the class, send the pitch, clean the space.
5. Repeat daily, because repetition is what transforms a wish into a new reality.

The Loophole: Your Brain Can't Tell the Difference

Your brain doesn't know the difference between imagination and memory. When you vividly visualize your ideal life, you activate the same neural pathways as if you're living it. Pair that visualization with the emotional signature of already having it, and your subconscious starts to accept it as truth.

From there, your behavior, tone, and energy naturally shift to match the new identity. The outside world responds accordingly.

Default Drift vs. Intentional Flow

Heraclitus said, *"You cannot step into the same river twice."* Life is always flowing. You are either:

- Drifting with default patterns, replaying the same thoughts, emotions, and choices as yesterday, getting the same results.
- Sculpting the current with intention, redirecting the flow toward what you want, not just what you've known.

Conscious creation is simply choosing the second option, over and over until it becomes second nature.

Alchemy in Action

Alchemy is transformation by design. In conscious creation, it looks like this:

- Fear arises, and it will.
- Instead of obeying it, you observe it. You recognize it as the echo of old wiring, not the voice of truth.
- You greet it like an old mentor who's outlived its role: *"You had your purpose. Now I write the next chapter."*

That's the moment the current changes. That's when you become the sculptor instead of the stone.

The Universe Is Always Listening

Every choice you make is a broadcast. The energy behind it tells the universe, *This is who I am, this is what I allow, and this is what I'm ready for.*

If your actions and energy say "scarcity," the universe matches it with lack.
If they say "abundance," the universe matches it with flow.
You don't "hope" for a better life, you become the person who already lives it.

Your 21-Day Reality Reset

Try this for 21 days and watch the shift:

1. Morning Visualization – 5 minutes of seeing and feeling your highest self.
2. Aligned Action – At least one step each day toward that self's life.
3. Energy Check-Ins – Throughout the day, pause and ask: *Is my energy matching what I want to attract?*
4. Night Script – Write down your ideal day as if it already happened.
5. Gratitude Lock-In – End each night naming 3 things you're grateful for *in advance*.

Wand in hand. World unfolding.

Conscious creation isn't magic, it's repetition, frequency, and faith in motion.

The current is yours to sculpt.

Raising Your Alchemical Frequency

Now that you know your energy is the instrument, the alchemist's true work is tuning it. Not once, but constantly, like a master violinist who checks the pitch before every note, or a sailor who adjusts the sails with every change of wind.

This isn't about spiritual perfection, it's about energetic hygiene.

Tending to your frequency is daily care, just like brushing your teeth, watering your plants, or clearing clutter from your space. It's part discipline, part flow, a spiritual rhythm that helps keep your internal world aligned. When your energy is clean and your system is tuned, the external world starts to reflect that clarity. Stay in integrity with your vibration, and life begins to meet you at your highest signal.

The Physics of Vibration

Every thought you think, every word you speak, every choice you make sends out a signal. That signal (your frequency) isn't abstract. It's measurable in your brainwaves, in the electromagnetic field around your heart, in the posture of your body, even in the micro-expressions on your face.

- When you dwell in gratitude, your heart's electromagnetic field becomes more coherent. This coherence boosts immune function, sharpens intuition, and improves emotional regulation.
- When you choose a thought of courage over fear, you trigger a cascade of neurotransmitters, dopamine, serotonin, that tell your nervous system, *We are safe, we are capable.*
- When you let go of toxic noise and tune into your own inner signal, you quiet the amygdala's alarm system and give your prefrontal cortex, the CEO of your brain, the space to lead.

This is the science behind what mystics have always known: your state creates your fate.

Micro-Adjustments, Macro-Results

Every high-vibe action you take is a micro-adjustment to your frequency:

- Saying "thank you" with sincerity.
- Taking 5 conscious breaths when you'd normally scroll.
- Dimming toxic noise to hear your own signal.
- Choosing a thought that lifts instead of loops.
- Walking barefoot to remember the Earth still holds you.
- Drinking water like it's liquid light.
- Closing your eyes to hear your soul before you hear the crowd.

Small acts are not small when repeated, they're the alchemical drops that shift the entire potion.

The Morning Compass Ritual

This simple, soul-shifting ritual is one of the most powerful practices I've found, and it started by accident.

One day, in a moment of exhaustion and prayer, I reached into a little box of words I had collected, tiny slips of paper, each holding a single intention: Grace. Trust. Courage. Stillness. I pulled one. Then another the next day. And the next.

At first, it felt small. Almost silly. But over time, something incredible happened.

As I journaled on my word each day, they began to tell a story. A quiet unfolding. One week, I pulled "Surrender," "Patience," "Grieve," "Trust," "Hope," "Rise," and then, finally, "Joy." It was like the universe was sending me breadcrumbs through the fog, guiding me from breakdown to rebirth, one word at a time.

It grounded me. Focused me. Inspired me. It gave me hope when I couldn't find my footing. That one word became a tiny beacon of meaning throughout my day.

Now, it's part of my daily rhythm, and it's become something others reach for too. I've had friends call me just to ask, *"What's our word today?"* Because sometimes, it's not the grand gestures that shift your path, it's the smallest acts of devotion that crack you open.

Let this become a sacred moment in your morning. It takes seconds, but its ripple is profound.

Try this daily reset:

1. **Choose One Word** – Peace. Radiance. Courage. Love. Or let it choose you.
2. **Journal a quick reflection** – What does this word mean to you today? What does it ask of you? Write freely, even if it's just a few lines.
3. **Let that word be your compass** – Return to it when the noise gets loud.
4. **Speak it aloud** – Especially when your energy dips.
5. **Write it down** – In your journal, on a sticky note, in the margins of your to-do list.
6. **Let it anchor your presence** – Until it hums quietly beneath your interactions, decisions, and energy.

That word?
It's not just your intention.
It's your frequency setting.
A small spark that can light your entire day.

The Law of Attraction Meets Alchemy

The Law of Attraction isn't just "think good thoughts." It's the
principle that frequency precedes form, that the vibration you emit
dictates the reality you inhabit.

In alchemy, the process is transmutation, turning lead into gold. In life,
your "lead" is fear, shame, and scarcity; your "gold" is confidence, joy,
and abundance. You don't just imagine the gold, you embody it until
the lead can't survive in your system anymore.

Every "no" to what drains you is an act of transmutation.
Every rewired thought is lead dissolving in the crucible.
Every time you speak life over your dream, you drop gold into the mix.

You Are the Alchemist

Let this be your vow, whispered between you and the universe:

I am the alchemist.
I do not shrink from the fire.
I am the fire.
I do not fear the dark.
I light it up.

You are not here to heal and hide. You are here to embody the shift so
completely that it's impossible not to feel your presence when you
walk into a room. This is the deeper Glow Up. This is spiritual maturity
with grit in its bones and fire in its eyes.

You are not bound by pain, you are empowered to transmute it.
You are not stuck, you are sculpting.
You are not fragile, you are forged.

And no one, not your past, not your fear, not even the quiet voice of doubt, gets to shape this life but you.

The Final Spark

As Heraclitus reminds us: "The fire within shapes all."

So shape it, alchemist.
Tend to it like the rarest flame.
Fuel it with gratitude, with courage, with truth.
And let your radiance be so potent, so unapologetic, that you can't help but light up the world.

CHAPTER 9

Embracing the Void – Healing Through Unimaginable Tragedy

For some, tragedy is not a single chapter, it's an entire volume rewritten in blood, silence, and memory.

It is not a surface scratch; it is the earthquake that cracked the foundation, the night that refused to end, the heartbreak that hollowed you out and left you wondering if you would ever recognize yourself again.

If your life has been marked by a loss so unimaginable it defies language, a child taken too soon, a body violated, a partner vanished, a dream shattered beyond recognition, know this: you are not invisible. You are seen. You are held.

The ache you carry is not a weakness. The way your breath catches without warning, how joy feels foreign or even forbidden, and how your skin remembers things you never asked it to hold? These are not instances of you "failing to move on." They are the truths of trauma's aftermath. You are not here to "get over it." You are here to learn how to live alongside it. To carry it with honor. To let light find the cracks without erasing the dark.

Trauma is not only an emotional wound, it is a physical one. The body stores what the mind cannot process.

Neuroscience shows that overwhelming experiences leave their fingerprints on the brain: the amygdala becomes overactive; the prefrontal cortex, your reasoning center, can go dim; the hippocampus, which helps file memories in the past, becomes compromised, leaving you feeling as if the worst moment of your life is still happening.

This isn't all in your head. It's in your fascia, your muscles, your breath, the tightness in your throat, the ache in your chest. Trauma is a full-body event, and healing must also be a full-body process.

This is where somatic healing becomes vital. "Somatic" simply means "of the body," and these practices help your nervous system, not just your conscious mind, learn that it is safe again. Language lives in the thinking brain, but trauma lives in sensation, impulse, and reflex.

It is stored as tension and shutdown. That's why a smell, a sound, or even a facial expression can trigger a flood of fear before you've even had a chance to think.

Somatic healing works by letting the body finish what was interrupted. Fight. Flee. Tremble. Cry. Freeze and then thaw. These are not dramatics, they are biology.

Practices like shaking, sighing, crying, grounding, and slow exhalations help release the charge. They let the nervous system complete the stress cycle it once had to suppress.

This is why placing your hand over your heart and whispering "I am still here" matters. Why walking barefoot or breathing into your belly can be medicine. Why one long, trembling sigh can release what words never could.

When Movement Isn't Possible

But what if your body *cannot* respond?
What if your trauma lives in a body that no longer moves, or only moves in fragments?

I want to speak directly to you.

I have not lived that loss myself. But I have walked closely beside it. I sit on the board of *Walking With Anthony*, a foundation committed to helping those living with spinal cord injuries reclaim hope, resources, and quality of life. I've seen firsthand what it means to lose function but not lose *purpose*. I've witnessed the courage of parents, caregivers, and survivors whose stories redefined resilience. I'm also actively involved in *Miracles for Kids*, supporting children facing life-altering illness, disability, and injury.

So while I have not lived your story, I have stood beside it. I believe you. I honor you. And I will never write you out of the healing conversation.

For those whose bodies cannot shake or run or scream, *your healing lives elsewhere*, but it is no less powerful.

Here's where you can begin:

1. Sound Healing + Breath

When movement isn't possible, sound becomes a gateway. Music, mantras, tones, singing bowls, chants, and even the vibration of your own voice can release trauma held deep within.

- Listen to binaural beats or solfeggio frequencies.
- Hum or sing (even softly). The vibration stimulates the vagus nerve and calms the body.
- Try coherent breathing: inhale for 4, exhale for 6. Let your body do what it can.
  Even the act of listening, intentionally, can rewire and regulate your nervous system.

2. Mental Rehearsal & Visualization

Neuroscience shows the brain responds to imagined movement almost as powerfully as physical action. This is called "motor imagery."

- Visualize yourself walking, dancing, swimming.
- Picture your cells healing, your energy recalibrating, your body bathed in light.
- Speak affirmations aloud, anchoring your mind in possibility.

These aren't just "positive thoughts." This is neuroplastic healing. Your mind is still a force.

3. Sacred Stillness & Witnessing

When movement is not an option, being fully present with your emotions becomes a ritual. Let yourself *feel* without moving to fix.

- Ask: What wants to be heard today?
- Journal what arises.
- Light a candle. Create a sensory ritual, a scent, a sound, a touch that signals *you are safe.*

Stillness is not passivity. It is presence. It is power.

4. Find the Mirrors

Healing is amplified within a community, especially among those who "get it."

- Seek out online groups, forums, or nonprofits centered around your lived experience.
- Listen to the stories of others who've found purpose through loss.
- Let your story be part of someone else's rising.

Whether you choose to speak or just be seen, belonging is a healing force. You are not alone.

Five Somatic Practices for the Darkest Days

There are moments when grief becomes too big for words.

Moments when the pain isn't a thought or a memory you can process, it is a full-body experience. Your chest tightens. Your breath shortens. Your nervous system shuts down or spirals into chaos. You're not "overreacting." You're overwhelmed.

These five somatic practices are not here to fix your pain. They're here to help you survive the wave, to bring your body enough relief to keep going. Think of them as sacred disruptions. Invitations back into your skin. Gentle ways to remind your system: I am still here. I am still safe. I am still moving forward.

You don't need to do them all. You don't need to do them perfectly. Let your body choose what feels doable. Let your grief be your teacher.

1. The Hand Over Heart Anchor

When you feel like you're floating outside yourself, this practice brings you home.

Sit or lie down in a quiet space. Place one hand over your heart and the other on your belly. Inhale through your nose for four counts. Feel the rise beneath your hands. Exhale slowly for six counts, letting your shoulders drop. Repeat for a few rounds.

If your mind is racing, whisper to yourself: *I am still here. I am still here.*

2. The Shaking Release

When energy builds and has nowhere to go, give your body a way out.

Stand with your feet shoulder-width apart, arms loose, knees soft. Begin to shake, hands, arms, shoulders, hips, legs. Let the movement ripple through you like a wave. Imagine the pain leaving your body like dust shaken from cloth.

Even two minutes can shift your energy. Sighs, yawns, or tears may follow, your body's way of saying: *Thank you.*

3. Grounding with the Earth

When you feel untethered, connect to something ancient beneath you.

If you can, step outside barefoot. If not, simply press your feet firmly into the floor. Imagine roots growing from your soles deep into the earth. With each inhale, draw strength up from below. With each exhale, release your weight down.

Let the earth carry what you can't. You are held.

4. The Scream You Never Gave

When the ache in your chest feels like pressure with no release, give it sound.

Find a private space, your car, the shower, or a pillow. Inhale deeply, and let out whatever comes: a scream, a sob, a growl. Don't worry about how it sounds. This isn't about performance, it's about permission.

This is not losing control.
This is giving your body the release it never got when it needed it most.

5. The Smallest Yes

When everything feels impossible, start small.

Drink a glass of water. Open a window. Step into the light for thirty seconds. These may feel insignificant, but they are not. Each small "yes" tells your nervous system: *Life is still happening. I am still part of it.*

Small yes's grow into bigger ones. One breath, one movement, one choice at a time.

After the Wave Passes

These practices won't erase your grief, but they will help you carry it differently.
They're not meant to heal everything. They're meant to soften the edge.
To make space inside your body so the pain doesn't take up all the air.

If you feel more grounded, more present, or simply able to breathe again, that is enough.

Grief doesn't always arrive as sadness. Sometimes it shows up as rage: sharp, hot, alive. Sometimes as numbness. Sometimes as a flood of tears. Every expression is valid.

Rage is sacred and it means something mattered. It's the echo of your boundaries, your love, your humanity. It can be released through movement, sound, stomping, running, or hitting a pillow until your arms give out.

Tears are sacred too. They hold wisdom. Contrary to what many people think, crying doesn't make you weak. It is a necessary release. Biologically, emotional tears carry stress hormones out of the body. Spiritually, they soften the armor around your heart.

And when your grief tells you to "be strong," remember:
Sometimes the bravest thing you can do is crumble.

Write the letter. Hold the photo. Let the sobbing come in waves until you are emptied enough to feel your breath again. This is not regression. This is repair.

Resilience is not resistance.
You can be strong and still shake.
You can be healing and still have days where getting out of bed is the victory.

Grief doesn't need to be erased. It wants to be integrated. To become part of your story without becoming the whole story.

Your joy, when it returns, will not be a betrayal.
It will be a resurrection.

Some days, rebirth is monumental. You'll speak your truth, start the memoir, build the foundation. Other days, it's brushing your teeth, making tea, stepping into the light.
All of it counts.
All of it is sacred.

One day, you may find yourself holding a lantern made from the very fire you thought would destroy you, and lifting it for someone still lost in the dark.

You don't have to be fully healed to help.
You only have to be real.

And when the memories come back like floodwaters, when you wonder if you'll ever laugh without guilt, remember:
Healing is not forgetting.
Joy is not disloyalty.
Your glow is not disrespectful to the darkness, it's proof you survived it.

You are living evidence that even in the void, a new world can be born. And your existence, scarred, glowing, still breathing, is its own kind of miracle.

CHAPTER 10

Unveiling Your Inner Mystic – Awakening Your Spiritual Power of Manifestation

Walk with me. Step into a starlit desert, where the night sky unfurls like a tapestry of cosmic dreams, each star a thread in the loom of your soul's infinite design. The air hums with secrets, sharp and alive, whispering truths that could unravel the universe itself. This is where you unveil your inner mystic, not a fleeting fantasy, but a radiant force that weaves your pain into purpose, your doubts into destiny.

You are not merely a body or a mind; you are a spark of the divine, a creator whose imagination shapes reality itself. This chapter is your sacred invitation to listen to your soul's quiet voice, to dance with the universe's boundless energy, and to embody the self you were born to become.

With a fire of cosmic clarity, we'll blend ancient wisdom, modern insight, and the mind-bending teachings of Neville Goddard, a mid-20th-century mystic and lecturer known for his radical insights on imagination, consciousness, and reality creation. Goddard saw imagination as the loom where your reality is woven.

At The Glow Up Project, we want you to remember that your soul is a star, and its light weaves the world, dreams boldly, and the universe bows.

You Are the Loom

Your spirit is a cosmic loom, threading every thought, every breath, into the fabric of your life. Long before the world measured truth in data, humans across cultures turned inward to access wisdom beyond logic.

In ancient Greece, seekers traveled to the Oracle of Delphi, where the priestess known as the *Pythia* entered trance-like states in Apollo's temple to deliver divine insight, visions that shaped empires and guided kings. Across the sacred landscapes of Australia, Aboriginal Dreamtime walkers followed ancestral songlines, pathways that mapped creation, spirit, and geography all at once. They understood that each step was a stitch in the universe's unfolding design.

These were not merely rituals or myths. They were technologies of the unseen, ways of engaging imagination, consciousness, and inner vision as forces that shaped reality itself.

Neville Goddard stepped into this same lineage of inner mysticism in the twentieth century, though he wore no ceremonial robes, and stood in lecture halls instead of temples. His message was simple, radical, and unsettling: imagination is not fantasy, it is divine. According to Goddard, consciousness is the only reality, and what you accept as true within must eventually express itself without. Where oracles sought visions from the gods, Goddard taught that *you are the divine dreamer*, shaping your world not through effort, but through assumption.

"Imagination," he wrote, "is the very gateway of reality." To feel the wish fulfilled before it appears is not pretending, it is creation.

Your thoughts are not idle. They are threads. They are instructions. They are blueprints. To awaken your inner mystic is to claim this power and to live from the end of your desire, to embody the self you long to be before the evidence arrives.

Picture a moment when you sensed a truth before logic caught up, a gut feeling to choose a new path, a quiet nudge to pause. That is your intuition, your soul's compass, weaving patterns faster than the sharpest mind can calculate. Modern research now confirms what mystics always knew: moments of deep presence and inner connection calm the nervous system, align the body, and restore clarity.

Sit for five minutes quietly, and ask, "What is my soul's truth today?" Let the answer arrive as it will, a fleeting image, a word, a warmth.

Whisper, "I am guided," and feel your inner rhythm steady. This is your mystic's first act: to imagine truth as if it is already real.

Weaving with the Universe

Your soul does not weave alone. It is threaded into a vast cosmic current that flows through stars, oceans, and the quiet rhythm of your breath. Goddard taught that you do not observe reality from the outside, you participate in it. You co-create not as a bystander, but as a conscious partner.

Imagine a golden thread stretching from your heart into the heavens. For three minutes, breathe deeply and repeat, "I weave with love." Step into nature, barefoot on grass, face tilted toward the sky, and whisper, "I am part of the whole."

The wind, the trees, and the stars are not separate from you. Ancient Taoists called this alignment with the Tao, the effortless flow that emerges when resistance dissolves. This is not escapism. It is authorship.

When doubt appears, consciously cancel the thought. Your soul is not here to doubt, It is here to weave.

Embodied Divinity

Your divinity is not a prize to earn. It is a truth to inhabit.

You are a fragment of the infinite, a star whose light requires no permission. Goddard urged us to live as if our desired self already exists, to feel confidence, worth, and joy *now*, not later.

Stand before a mirror and say, "I am divine. I am whole." Let the words settle. Or pour your divinity into creation, draw, write, dance. Let imagination move through your body.

Focus intently on true embodiment.

Plotinus described the soul as a divine emanation, forever linked to the One. Your pain, your fear, your longing, they are not flaws. They are pigments in the masterpiece you are becoming.

If self-doubt whispers, let it pass. Your divinity is not up for debate.

The Mystic's Practice

To sustain this awakening, weave it into your days gently, intentionally.

Once a week, act on a gut instinct. Monthly, explore a new spiritual practice. Share your light freely, through presence, laughter, truth. Read Goddard not as doctrine, but as ignition. Let these teachings spark remembrance. They are threads. And with them, you weave a reality where your desired self is no longer imagined, it is lived.

"Assume the feeling of the wish fulfilled," Goddard taught, "and your world will conform." Your inner mystic is not a phase or a fantasy. It is the eternal flame no darkness can extinguish. Each time you trust your intuition, embody your divinity, or imagine boldly, you are shaping the world from the inside out.

I've often been told my head is in the clouds, or that I don't live in "reality."

To that, I smile and say, "It's beautiful up here." [wink]

But in all honesty: this isn't about floating away. This is about grounding your vision into form. It's about walking through the real world with soul-led steps, clear eyes, and a heart tuned to higher wisdom.

This is not escape. This is sacred engagement.

Your soul is a star. Its light weaves the world.

Dream boldly and let the universe respond.

Becoming the Highest Version of You

Now that your mystic is awake, alive, radiant, burning with possibility, I invite you to step back into the sacred fire of transformation. Becoming your highest self is not a destination. It is a frequency. A remembrance. Your lowest point is the doorway to your highest self. Embrace the darkness. For only in the absence of light, do we learn to become the light.

You already carry the blueprint. The divine lives in your breath, your laughter, your vision.

And now, we bring it into form.

CHAPTER 11

Radiance Unleashed – Living as Your Highest Self

You are the alchemist, the poet, the architect of a new reality, one that radiates with such authenticity and purpose, it becomes impossible to ignore. You are no longer walking a path of repair, but a path of revelation, and what you reveal is pure, cosmic brilliance.

The mind seeks comfort, but the soul yearns for change, for growth. When you experience pain, sit with it. Listen. When you emerge again, you will realize the joy was never in the outcome, but in the transformation.

This chapter is your portal to radical authenticity, collective healing, and legacy-building. We will explore the sacred balance between flow and surrender, the mystical rhythm where time dissolves and your essence speaks louder than your ego. Here, ancient wisdom dances with modern science. Here, your radiance becomes a ripple effect that shifts the frequency of everything around you.

This is about breaking down completely and rebuilding yourself back stronger. It's about unleashing a radiance so authentic, so purposeful, it rewrites the path of your life.

Your radiance is no fleeting spark, it's a cosmic tide, reshaping the world with every wave.

Radical Authenticity: You, Undiluted

Your highest self isn't polished, it's powerful. It isn't perfect, it's present. Radical authenticity asks you to drop the masks, the performances, and the societal scripts. To stand in your truth, even when your voice trembles. Even when the world expects you to play small.

Every time you tell the truth of who you are, you reclaim a piece of your soul. Every time you say no to what drains you and yes to what lights you up, you become more whole, and true happiness is a byproduct of becoming whole.

And guess what? The world doesn't need more copies. It needs your frequency, raw, rare, and real.

Sit quietly and ask yourself: Where am I still shrinking? What dream have I tucked away for the sake of being "realistic?" Then, take one sacred, bold, messy step in that direction. Maybe it's a dream to change paths or a desire to speak boldly. Say it aloud, let it hum through you like a note struck on a tuning fork, take one small step, research a new venture, voice a quiet wish, watch your days transform.

You don't owe anyone a watered-down version of your light. As *The Glow Up Project* reminds us: "Your truth is your throne, claim it, and the world bows to your light."

Radical authenticity is more than a concept, it's a practice. It's writing the poem you have hidden, admitting the dream that scares you, wearing what makes your spirit hum, or speaking your truth even if your voice shakes. It's no longer waiting for permission. It's permission itself.

When you live like this, you don't just inspire, you awaken. You give others the silent nod to show up as they are. You become the living proof that freedom is possible.

And in a world addicted to polished personas, your rawness becomes sacred rebellion.

This is where you stop dimming to be digestible. Where you become the mirror that shows others their truth is safe, sacred, and meant to shine.

Collective Healing: Your Glow Heals Others

Your radiance doesn't end with you, it's a wave that ripples outward, lifting the collective like a tide raising all ships. Ancient traditions, from Indigenous healing circles to Buddhist sanghas, knew that shared transformation amplifies light, weaving hearts into a collective of connection.

Your authentic truth, when shared, becomes a spark that ignites others. Try joining a small circle with friends, a book club, a tribe of seekers, and share one honest intention: "I'm learning to trust my path." Listen deeply, affirming another's truth, and feel the collective energy rise like a chorus finding harmony.

Or simply offer a smile, a kind word, to a stranger, and watch their eyes light up. This isn't just connection; it's co-creation, a dance where your glow kindles others'.

Surrender here is key; release the need to control outcomes, trust the universe to carry your light. Stand in nature, breathe deeply, and whisper, "My radiance flows freely." Let go of how it lands, like a poet releasing a verse to the wind. Your healing, when shared, becomes a gift, a thread in the collective's luminous weave.

One candle doesn't lose its flame by lighting another, and neither will you.

You heal the world by daring to shine unapologetically. Even your quietest truths are powerful in motion.

The more you live your truth, the more you anchor permission into the field. You're not just part of the collective, you're reshaping it.

Legacy in Motion: Creating from the Soul

The highest self doesn't just live for today. It plants seeds for a tomorrow it may never see.

Your legacy is being written in every act of courage, every creation born of love, every truth spoken in the face of fear. It's not about building empires, it's about building energy that echoes, lasts, and heals.

The ancient Egyptian concept of *ma'at*, living in harmony with truth, saw every choice as a ripple in the cosmic order. Your legacy is the light you leave in others' hearts, whether through a story you share, a kindness you offer, or a creation you birth.

Spend ten minutes daily dreaming. What mark do you wish to leave? Perhaps it's a project, a lesson, or a moment of inspiration. Take one step, outline a chapter, volunteer, teach a skill, and feel your purpose expand like a starfield unfurling.

Legacy isn't always loud. Sometimes it's the handwritten note, the laughter of your children, the way your energy lingers in a room long after you leave. It's the teacher who shifted your trajectory. It's the healer whose words made you cry. Now, you get to be that for someone else.

Write the book. Paint the mural. Start the garden. Say the thing. Your highest self isn't waiting to leave a mark, it already is.

Every moment lived in truth is a legacy in motion.

Flow and Surrender: The Dance of Divine Radiance

Flow is presence in motion.
Surrender is presence in trust.
Together, they create radiance.

We spend so much of life trying to control outcomes, timelines, people, emotions. We grip tightly to expectations because chaos feels threatening. Control, we believe, is safety. But what if the control we crave is the very thing that's keeping us stuck?

The Illusion of Control

Control is often just fear dressed up in discipline.
It's the ego's attempt to predict, protect, and produce results it *thinks* are necessary for survival, love, or success. But here's the secret: when we try to control everything, we block the divine.

We get tunnel vision.
We fixate on a single outcome.
And in doing so, we reject the 99 miracles that were trying to find us another way.

When you try to micromanage the universe, you become stuck in a state of waiting, waiting for the thing you *think* you need to be happy, to move forward, to exhale. You place your life on pause until that thing arrives.

But here's the medicine:
When you stop waiting, you drop the weight.
When you stop forcing, you start flowing.
When you stop chasing, you become magnetic.

What Flow *Really* Feels Like

Flow is not just a good day or a moment of peace, it's the full embodiment of presence.
It's the trance of creation.
The heartbeat of alignment.
The art of becoming the moment itself.

You find flow when:

- You create something that puts your soul in charge (music, painting, writing, cooking).
- You move your body in a way that makes you feel alive
- You speak, teach, or serve from your essence.
- You lose track of time because your soul has taken the reins.

In these moments, you are plugged into the source. You're not controlling, you're co-creating.

The Power (and Pain) of Surrender

Surrender is not giving up.
It's giving over.

It's choosing to believe that the Divine has a better GPS than your fear ever could.

Surrender is the art of letting go *before* you understand.
It's the act of unclenching your fists and whispering, "I trust."

It's knowing that the thing that dissolved wasn't your punishment, it was your redirection.

It hurts, sometimes.
We miss people. We mourn timelines. We resist the detours.
But often, the things that crumble were never built for the version of you that's coming.

The Art of Detachment: The Most Sacred Skill of All

Detachment doesn't mean apathy. It doesn't mean you stop caring or give up your dreams.

Detachment is freedom.
It's realizing that you can desire deeply while still releasing the outcome.
It's saying: "This or something better. I trust you, Divine."

When you learn detachment:

- You no longer chase, you attract.
- You no longer wait, you live.
- You no longer beg, you embody.

Detachment is the bridge between *manifestation* and *miracle*.

When you cling to one specific outcome, you delay divine delivery. You limit yourself to the vision of your current self instead of opening the path for your *evolved self* to receive what's actually aligned.

You Are the Frequency, Not the Force

Manifestation is not a hustle.
It's a frequency game.
You don't *get* what you want, you get what you are.

So ask yourself:

Who would I be if I already had this thing I desire?
How would I walk, speak, breathe, love, create?

Become that version.
Then release the timeline. Let the Divine reroute you as needed. That's flow. That's surrender.

Practices to Embody Flow and Surrender

Here are a few ways to integrate this truth into your everyday Glow:

Affirmations for Surrender

> "I trust the detours are divine."

> "I don't chase, I align."

> "What is for me cannot be missed."

Daily Detachment Ritual

> Write down what you want.

> Read it out loud with love.

> Burn it or bury it and walk away.

> Smile. It's done.

Flow Practice

> Block out one hour per week to *create* without expectation.

> Let yourself enter trance, write, paint, dance, build, run, garden.

> Notice how your energy shifts.

Remember: surrender isn't giving up, it's giving over. It's letting your highest self steer the ship.

Flow allows you to merge with the divine in real time. Surrender allows the divine to merge with you. Together, they form a feedback loop of expansion. When you're in flow, you're fully here. When you surrender, you trust what's next.

Flow is the art.
Surrender is the faith.
Radiance is the result.

So stop gripping.

You are not here to chase life.
You are here to become it.

Your Radiance Is Revolutionary

Living as your highest self is a radical act in a world addicted to conformity. It is an act of rebellion. Of healing. Of remembering. Every time you choose joy over guilt, authenticity over approval, presence over productivity, you radiate.

So let your glow be loud. Let it burn. Let it light the path for the next soul ready to rise.

You are no longer just becoming. You are now becoming *uncontainable*.

You are the living spell, the embodiment of every wish your ancestors whispered, the answer to your younger self's prayers.

You are the revolution.

The cycle breaker.

You are a legacy in motion. A radiant force in bloom. A soul that burns with purpose.

Your Turn: Radiance in Practice

For 5 minutes daily, practice a "soul's radiant tide" ritual:

- Stand tall.
- Breathe deeply.
- Choose one act, speak a truth, share a moment of connection, or create with purpose.
- Whisper, "My light flows free."
- Write one word after (e.g., "tide").

Once a week, take a bold step that feels like your highest self, share a dream, start a project, trust the flow.

Because your radiance is the revolution.

And it's already happening.

Just keep blazing.

CHAPTER 12

Nourishing Your Eternal Glow – Self-Care as Sacred Embodiment

You are a living temple, a vessel crafted by the divine, and to care for yourself is one of the most sacred acts of love you can offer. It's a ritual of remembrance. A declaration to the universe: *I am grateful. I am whole. I am worthy.*

After naming your pain, rising through trauma, and awakening your highest self, you arrive at the altar of embodiment. Here, self-care becomes something far deeper than routine. It is devotion. It is presence. It is a vow to honor the vessel that carries your soul and to nourish your being from the inside out.

In this chapter, you will learn how to treat every act of care, physical, emotional, and spiritual, as a holy invocation of your truth. An essential way of being. This is your guide to tending your human vessel, becoming so attuned and intentional in your daily routine that your glow becomes undeniable.

Through the practices in this chapter, you will deepen your relationship with yourself and begin to live as the embodied expression of your light. Together, we'll explore six sacred pillars of self-devotion:

- **Mindful Nutrition** – honoring your body through nourishment that supports vitality and energy.
- **Joyful Movement** – reconnecting to the pleasure of being alive in your body.
- **Sacred Adornment** – expressing your inner essence through intentional beauty and self-expression.
- **Daily Glow Rituals** – grounding your spirit through practices that bring you back to center.

- **Community Anchoring** – cultivating relationships that mirror your worth and hold you in your becoming.
- **Generational Legacy** – reclaiming your healing as a gift to those who came before and those who will follow.

Each of these is more than a practice, it is a declaration. A way of turning the everyday into the extraordinary. A life where every choice becomes a prayer and every breath becomes a blessing.

Mindful Nutrition: Feeding Your Divine Essence

Your body is the altar. And food? Food is the offering. Every bite that you take is an energetic signature. A message to your cells. A yes to life.

Think of this as a sacred structure: flexible, loving, and designed to support your glow. This is about feeding your divine essence. Choosing foods that honor your energy, your rhythm, your radiance.

Ancient Ayurvedic teachings viewed food as prana; a life force. And modern science backs it: nourishing your body with whole, colorful, nutrient-rich meals stabilizes your hormones, uplifts your mood, and enhances your glow.

Let your meals become rituals. Chop mindfully. Cook with joy. Infuse each bite with presence. Bless your food with a whisper: "I feed my soul."

And when old patterns arise (the rush, the mindless snacking, the skipping) pause. Return to reverence. Your body deserves slowness. She deserves color. She deserves care.

When you eat with love, you vibrate with life.

The Chemistry of Conscious Eating

Food isn't just fuel, it's information. What you put into your body communicates directly with your brain, hormones, and nervous system.

Deficiencies in key nutrients, like magnesium, omega-3s, B12, vitamin D, zinc, and amino acids, can manifest as anxiety, depression, irritability, and even symptoms of psychosis. (Always consult with a qualified healthcare provider to understand your individual needs before starting any new supplements or nutritional protocols.)

Your gut is your second brain, housing over 90% of your serotonin and producing neurotransmitters that regulate your mood, sleep, focus, and resilience. A dysregulated gut from years of processed foods, antibiotics, alcohol, and stress will speak back to you in panic attacks, brain fog, and fatigue.

You are not just what you eat. You are what your body *can absorb*.

A Nutritional Map Through the Ages

In Your 20s:

- Focus on building habits and stabilizing hormones.
- Key nutrients: Omega-3s, iron (especially for menstruating women), B-complex, magnesium.
- Supplement support: Probiotics, vitamin D, adaptogens like ashwagandha (with professional guidance).

In Your 30s:

- Prioritize hormonal balance, gut health, and cellular repair.
- Add in collagen, antioxidants, CoQ10, and fermented foods.
- Begin tracking your body's response to food (e.g. energy, inflammation).

In Your 40s and Beyond:

- Support declining hormones, brain health, and bone density.
- Prioritize calcium, magnesium, D3, K2, and high-quality proteins.
- Consider hormone-balancing herbs like maca, and bioavailable multivitamins.

Again, always consult with a functional medicine doctor or certified professional before beginning any new supplement regimen.

How Depletion Affects the Mind

When your body lacks nutrients, it doesn't just affect your waistline, it affects your worldview. Depletion can mimic depression. Low blood sugar can trigger panic. Chronic inflammation from processed food can cause mood swings, memory issues, and chronic exhaustion. When your physical vessel is struggling, your spirit can't soar.

Balancing your blood sugar, hydrating your cells, and replenishing your minerals is not just "health advice", it's energetic alignment.

You can't heal emotionally when your brain is starving.

Alcohol, Sleep, and Your Nervous System

Let's talk about alcohol.

It may feel like a social lubricant or a numbing balm, but the truth is, it robs your nervous system of stability. Alcohol disrupts REM cycles, depletes B vitamins, strips the gut lining, and floods your brain with rebound anxiety. One night of drinking can reduce sleep quality by over 70%, which impacts memory, emotional regulation, and healing.

This isn't about shame. It's about sovereignty. Know how it affects you, and then *choose* consciously.

The Divine Healing Formula

Healing is never one-size-fits-all, but here are foundational practices that nourish every body:

- Eat real, whole foods that come from the earth.
- Cook more than you order.
- Eat fresh fruits & vegetables that are in season.
- Hydrate with mineral-rich water (consider trace mineral drops).
- Focus on adding *more* of what nourishes, not just subtracting "bad" foods.
- Avoid overly restrictive diets unless medically necessary, they can dysregulate your nervous system.

Mindful nutrition is not about being perfect. It's about being aware.

Final Thoughts: Feed to Heal

Let your plate be a prayer. Let your food be an act of love. Let your healing be holistic, mind, body, and soul.

Because when you eat with awareness, your body feels safe. And a safe body is a body that can heal.

Nourish to rise. Feed your frequency. And remember, your glow begins within.

Joyful Movement: Celebrating Your Body's Song

Your body was meant to be treasured.
It was meant to be celebrated. To move. To breathe. To dance with the earth and sweat your truth back into your skin.
Joyful movement is a love letter to your body. Burning calories is great but it is the intention behind the movement that really matters. Releasing stagnation. Inviting ecstasy. Expanding. Getting turned on by life.

Movement is how we commune with the divine housed in muscle and bone. Whether it's a sway in the kitchen, a barefoot walk on grass, a sweaty dance party, or a soulful stretch, movement is how you say to your body: *"I love you, Thank you"*

The Science of Sacred Movement

On a physiological level, movement is a catalyst. Regular physical activity increases levels of serotonin and dopamine, the very neurotransmitters that boost your mood, focus, and resilience. It lowers cortisol, stabilizes blood sugar, and supports the lymphatic system in clearing toxins from the body.

Even five minutes of intentional movement has been shown to:

- Improve memory and cognitive function

- Lower inflammation
- Increase oxygen flow to the brain
- Regulate circadian rhythms
- Activate vagus nerve tone, enhancing nervous system balance

When you move with joy and intention, you're not just burning calories, you're wiring your brain for vitality.

Trauma, The Body, and Movement as Release

Trauma isn't just in your mind, it's in your muscles, your fascia, your breath pattern.
The body remembers what the mind tries to forget.

That's why movement is so critical to trauma healing. It literally *shakes* old energy loose. Practices like:

- Qigong help regulate your energy body and restore flow.
- Rebounding (mini trampoline) activates lymphatic drainage and emotional release.
- Ecstatic dance allows repressed feelings to rise and transmute through rhythm.
- Walking meditations rewire the nervous system through forward movement and intentional presence.

Each time you move mindfully, you are saying to your nervous system:
"It's safe to be here now."

Movement as Ritual

Let your workouts become rituals.
Light a candle. Play music that stirs your soul.
Breathe with your movement. Cry if it comes. Laugh if it rises. Sigh if your spirit needs to exhale.

Be present, intentional, determined.

Movement Across the Ages: What to Focus On

Your movement practice will evolve as you do.

In your 20s:

- Focus on building strong bones, muscle tone, and body awareness.
- Mix strength training with cardio and mobility.
- Avoid overtraining. For women, prioritize menstrual cycle awareness and rest.

In your 30s:

- Balance high-intensity with recovery.
- Strengthen the pelvic floor, core, and posture.
- Support hormones with resistance training, but downshift during PMS or fatigue.

In your 40s and beyond:

- Shift toward functional fitness, joint mobility, and nervous system support.
- Walking, swimming, pilates, yoga, tai chi, rebounding, and resistance bands are your allies.
- Recovery becomes as important as intensity. Think: strong *and* soft.

There is no age where movement should be about punishment. Only reverence.

Joyful Movement for Mental Health

If you struggle with anxiety or depression, movement becomes your daily medicine.
Not as a chore, but as an anchor.

Walking, dancing, stretching, even for 10 minutes, can:

- Reduce cortisol and adrenaline
- Boost endorphins

- Clear mental fog
- Interrupt ruminating thought loops
- Re-establish a rhythm in the body-mind

And if you're neurodivergent, dealing with PTSD, or navigating emotional overwhelm, gentle and repetitive motion, like rocking, swaying, or breath-led yoga, can soothe your nervous system.

You Don't Need to Be Perfect. You Just Need to Be Present.

Some days you'll feel like a warrior in the gym.
Other days you'll be stretching in your pajamas with one sock on and mascara tears on your tank top.
Both count.

This isn't about how many reps you did.
It's about how deeply you connected with your body in the process.

It's about building trust with your physical vessel, the one that carried you through trauma, heartbreak, and healing, and saying, "I choose joy with you now."

Intentional Self-Presentation: Adorning Your Sacred Canvas

You are art.
And the way you adorn yourself is sacred.
It is spellwork. It is ceremony. It is a reclamation of presence in a world that profits from your self-doubt.

When you choose to embody your essence through style, grooming, scent, and self-touch, you're not performing for approval, you're claiming who you are. You are telling your nervous system: *It's safe to be seen. I belong to myself now.*

Style as a Soul Language

The way you show up in the world is your energetic handshake. Before you speak a word, your energy introduces you, and your physical expression carries the message.

- That color you wear? It's vibration.
- That style choice? A mood made visible.
- That chain, jacket, ring, or cologne? Armor. Adornment. Identity.

This isn't about trends or the pressure to look "put together." This is about integrity, aligning your outer appearance with your inner truth. When you wear something that feels like an *affirmation*, you walk differently.
When you take the time to care for your skin, your hair, your nails, your breath, it tells your subconscious:
I am worthy of tending.

A Ritual, Not a Routine

Intentional self-presentation is more than getting dressed. It's a ritual. A moment of devotion between you and your vessel.

Try this:

- Light a candle before getting ready.
- Ask, "How do I want to feel today?" and dress from that energy.
- Touch your skin like it's precious, not a project.
- Spritz your favorite scent and imagine it sealing in your aura.

Let your bathroom become a temple. Your vanity, an altar. Your mirror, a portal of reverence.

When you look into your reflection and whisper, "I see you. I honor you," something in you softens. Your nervous system exhales. Your soul sits upright.

The History of Adornment: You Come From Ritual

Throughout time, humans have decorated their bodies as expressions of meaning, identity, and reverence.

- To prepare for battle.
- To honor a rite of passage.
- To embody a deity.
- To grieve or to celebrate.

You come from ancestors who understood that how you show up in your physical body shapes your energy field.

Adorning yourself is about sovereignty.
It says: I choose to live in my body with presence, power, and poise.

Grooming as Grounding

In moments of trauma, chaos, or depression, personal hygiene can slip. We stop tending. We go numb.
This is not laziness, it's nervous system overload. But reclaiming even one small act of care can shift everything.

- Washing your face becomes a reset button.
- Combing your hair becomes an act of self-respect.
- Moisturizing your skin becomes a return to embodiment.

Even if you're not "going anywhere", especially then, getting ready is healing.
Choose softness over shame. Go slowly. Let it be about energy, not effort.

The Aura of Authenticity

You don't need a designer wardrobe or 12-step skincare. You need authenticity.
Wear what makes you feel beautiful, bold, soft, alive, wild, grounded, royal, whatever truth your soul wants to wear that day.

Because when you are dressed in alignment with your essence, your aura expands. People feel it.

They don't know what it is, but they're drawn to it.

You are in your glow. Not just because of what's on your body, but because of how your soul is shining through it.

Adorning After Trauma: The Return to Self

For those healing from abuse, body shame, sexual trauma, or neglect, reclaiming your image can be confronting.

But it can also be revolutionary.

Adorning yourself becomes a radical act of saying:

- *This body is mine.*
- *This pleasure is mine.*
- *This reflection is a story still being written.*

You're allowed to flirt with your own reflection.

You're allowed to wear silk and oils and jewelry just because it makes you feel powerful.

You're allowed to enjoy your beauty without apology.

When the Mirror Becomes a Portal

Try this practice:

- Stand in front of a mirror.
- Lock eyes with yourself.
- Breathe deeply into your belly.
- Say aloud: "I honor my radiance."

Do this every day for 7 days. Watch what changes, not just in how you see yourself, but how you walk into the world.

Because you set the standard. When you treat yourself like a temple, others learn to treat you that way too.

Daily Radiance Practices: Kindling the Inner Ember

Your glow isn't luck, it's legacy. It's cultivated. Tended to. Nourished daily like an ember that never goes out.

Radiance is ritual. It's the five-minute gratitude practice. The cup of tea sipped in silence. The pause between tasks where you breathe and say, "I am alive, I am grateful."

Research shows that daily mindfulness practices literally rewire the brain for resilience, presence, and joy. Ancient Stoics understood this too, that daily rituals anchor the soul.

So choose a few sacred rhythms:

- Morning breathwork + mantra: "My light is steady."
- Midday gratitude list.
- Evening bath with oils + candlelight.
- Mirror work: whispering love into your own eyes.

These rituals are the language of self-respect.

Community Anchoring: Rooting Your Light in Love

Your radiance is amplified in connection. In laughter. In shared tears. In knowing glances that say, "I see you."

Community is your soul's mirror. It reflects your light when you forget. It holds you when your fire flickers. Ubuntu wisdom says, "I am because we are." Science echoes it, community strengthens immunity, lengthens lifespan, and lifts mood.

So join hands. Join circles. Reach out. Share your truth. Witness someone else's. Text a friend. Hug a stranger. Say thank you with your eyes.

Your glow was never just yours. It's contagious. It is a torch passed.

Generational Legacy: Passing the Flame

Your glow doesn't end with you.

Every time you care for yourself, you rewrite your lineage. Every time you rest instead of overwork, nourish instead of deprive, honor instead of shame, you heal generations.

Legacy is built in your rituals. In your laughter. In your strength. In the stories you pass down, the recipes you share, the energy you bring into every room.

Write a letter to your future children. Or your future self. Plant a seed. Start a tradition. Share a mantra. Leave a glow trail.

Because when you nourish yourself, you create a map for others to do the same.

Levinas reminds us: care is responsibility. And in caring for yourself, you are caring for the future.

Self-care is not a luxury. It is legacy. It is spiritual. It is political. It is revolutionary. When you rise with intention, nourish with reverence, and embody with love, you become magnetic elixir.

So let every bite, every step, every touch be sacred.

Whisper to yourself each morning: "I am a living temple. I rise in strength and radiance."

And may the world bask in your light.

CHAPTER 13

The Ripple Effect – Healing the World Through Your Light

Envision yourself as a lighthouse, your beam a prismatic tide that pierces the darkness, not merely guiding but revealing the hidden unity of all souls. Your healing is no solitary spark, it is a radiant wave, rippling through the collective, mending the fractures of a wounded world.

This chapter is your summons to rise, not as a survivor bound by pain, but as a healer whose light unveils the truth: we are all born of the same soul, mirrors of one another, transformed by the kaleidoscope of our experiences and perceptions.

Drawing from *The Four Agreements* by Don Miguel Ruiz, we see that your words, your freedom from others' judgments, your clarity beyond assumptions, and your unwavering effort weave a reality where oneness is not a dream but a lived truth. Your pain, those raw, jagged edges of loss or struggle, is not a chain but a prism, refracting your light to guide others.

With a philosopher's fire, we'll explore compassionate presence, sacred activism, and global connection, rooted in the science of mirror neurons and the psychology of collective consciousness, to reveal how your purpose transforms suffering into a beacon that heals the world.

*"Your light is the mirror of the infinite, reflecting one soul
in every heart,"*
—inspired wisdom from The Glow Up Project.

Compassionate Presence

Reflecting the Soul, Radiating the Medicine

Your healing is not just for you.
It is a vibration, a frequency, a pulse that echoes into the collective

field. When you shift, *we all feel it*. Your healing becomes an anchor. Your awakening becomes an invitation. Your compassion becomes a mirror.

Don Miguel Ruiz teaches that we are born as pure light, whole and untarnished. But quickly, we inherit the dream of the world, a set of agreements, projections, and perceptions that bury that light beneath layers of conditioning.

We are told who we are.
We are taught how to behave.
We absorb the shame, the fear, the judgments of others, and call them truth.

But they are not. And healing is remembering.

Compassionate Speech: Inspired by The First Agreement

Ruiz doesn't say "be nice." He says *be impeccable.*

That means being aligned. Honest. Clear. Rooted in integrity. Your words are spells (hence the word "spelling"). They shape how others feel and how you experience yourself.

To speak with love is not to sugarcoat, it's to honor the truth without weaponizing it. It's to use language as light.

In a world of gaslighting, gossip, and spiritual bypassing, being impeccable with your word is revolutionary. And when it's grounded in compassion? It becomes *healing energy in audible form.*

Let this be your mantra: "I do not use my voice to harm, manipulate, or shame. I use it to liberate."

The Mirror Principle: Seeing Self in Other

We often think compassion is about "being nice." But true compassion is *ferocious.* It is the fire that burns away illusion. It is the awareness that *we are all walking projections*, reflecting parts of ourselves onto each other.

That person you resent? Mirror.
That moment of jealousy? Mirror.
That stranger who warms your heart? Also mirror.

To live compassionately is to live with mirrored vision. You see
yourself *in everyone*. Not to excuse their behavior, but to dissolve the
illusion of separation.

The Ubuntu tradition says, *"I am because we are."*
It is more than a proverb, it is a cosmic law.
If you are healing, then I am healing.
If I am healing, then you are too.

Your Nervous System is Contagious

Dan Siegel's work in interpersonal neurobiology has proven what the
mystics always knew: our presence *regulates or dysregulates* others.

Your calm can calm the storm.
Your safety can anchor someone else's chaos.
Your self-awareness can create ripple effects through entire lineages.

When you sit with someone in pain and breathe slowly, without fixing,
without judging, you invite their nervous system to down-regulate.
This isn't abstract. It's biological. Mirror neurons fire. Oxytocin flows.
Cortisol drops. Hearts sync.

This is sacred work.
When you choose healing, presence, and truth, you become an
offering.
You stop cycles.
You change bloodlines.
You light up every room, not because you're loud, but because your
frequency speaks first.

The Agreements Are Pathways Back to Unity

Let's revisit the *Four Agreements*, not as ideals, but as energy portals:

1. **Be Impeccable With Your Word** – Speak from integrity. No gossip. No venom. Just soul-truth and sacred yes's. Use your voice to bless, not wound.
2. **Don't Take Anything Personally** – Everyone's projections are about *them*. Not you. Even the ones that hurt.
3. **Don't Make Assumptions** – Ask. Clarify. Stay curious. Judgment kills connection. Compassion feeds it.
4. **Always Do Your Best** – Your best today may be messy, tired, raw. That's okay. Grace lives here.

These aren't just concepts. They are spiritual armor. Emotional refinement. Compassion in action.

The Deeper Question: Who Are You Reflecting?

Every day, we reflect something; fear or faith, lack or love, judgment or presence.

So ask yourself:

- When I walk into a room, what ripples out from me?
- Do I make people feel safer or smaller?
- Am I projecting my pain, or holding space for transformation?

This is not about performance. It is about energy. It is about being *aware*.

Take 5 minutes each day. Breathe. Visualize your body like a mirror, wiped clean. Ask, "Who am I reflecting today?" Visualize your interactions as mirrors, are you casting light or shadows?

Compassion as Revolution

This world doesn't need more opinions. It needs more *presence*.
More people who can witness without fixing.
Listen without projecting.
Hold space without judgment.
Love without needing to be right.

You are not here to be everyone's healer.
But you are here to be the reflection of what healing *feels* like.

Be the frequency that reminds others of who they are.
Be the safe mirror in a world of distortion.
Be the presence that awakens the soul in someone who forgot they had one.

"When you see yourself in others, it is impossible to hurt them." – Thich Nhat Hanh

You Are the Medicine

When your presence is rooted in compassion, your very being becomes magnetic. People feel it. They trust you. And not because you fix them, but because you *see them*.

You become the mirror that reminds others they are already whole.
You reflect the soul.
You ripple love.
You heal the world, without even trying.

Sacred Activism

Healing Through Purpose

There comes a point in your healing journey when personal transformation is no longer enough. The pain you have alchemized becomes too potent to hold in isolation. The wisdom you've earned demands a direction. The fire in your belly says, *Now do something with it.*

That moment?
That's sacred activism.

Sacred activism is your soul's light in motion, a purposeful act that channels your pain into a force for transformation. Your struggles, those moments of doubt, grief, or isolation, are not flaws but facets of the same soul we all share, giving you a unique lens to heal the world.

These ripples become waves.
These waves become tides.
And tides reshape shores.

What Is Sacred Activism?

Coined by Andrew Harvey, spiritual scholar and thought leader, *sacred activism* is the fusion of deep spiritual practice with wise, radical action. It is when inner awakening meets outer change. Not activism rooted in anger, blame, or burnout, but in devotion, compassion, and fierce love.

It asks:

- What breaks your heart wide open?
- What injustice keeps you up at night?
- What gift, skill, or truth are you *uniquely* here to offer?

This isn't about becoming a martyr. It's about *alchemizing* your pain into purpose and letting that purpose ripple outward like light from a lantern.

> *"Your heartbreak is a roadmap. Your purpose lives there."*
> —The Glow Up Project

Your Pain Is a Compass

Most people think purpose comes from passion. But often, it comes from pain.

The death of someone you loved.
The childhood where you never felt safe.
The shame that silenced your voice.
The system that failed you.

You survived it.
Now what?

Sacred activism says: use it. Let your trauma teach. Let your ache serve. Let your scars become a map for others still lost in the woods.

Your suffering made you fluent in a language someone else is still learning. Your healing is their hope.

The Neuroscience of Purpose

Modern neuroscience affirms what the mystics always knew: purposeful action rewires the brain.

Studies show that when we engage in acts aligned with our core values, especially those that help others, we light up the brain's dopamine and serotonin centers. Purpose boosts the ventral striatum and prefrontal cortex, creating not just emotional fulfillment, but neurological resilience.

In simple terms: purpose heals the brain.
You glow differently when you know why you're here.

Healing Is a Ripple Effect

Every sacred act creates a wave. A smile. A donation. A boundary. A painting. A protest. A story. A truth. An apology. A poem. A prayer. These are not small. They are sacred. And they matter.

Start small. Pick one *Ripple Act* each week:

- Tell someone you believe in them.
- Share your story to help another find theirs.
- Advocate for a cause with your time, talent, or treasure.
- Write a post that liberates, not performs.
- Start a healing circle, a support group, or a mindful business.
- Send a meal. Light a candle. Show up.

Ancient and Modern Wisdoms

The Four Agreements reminds us that doing your best isn't about perfection, it's about showing up as the best version of yourself. It's about showing up for life, for others, for yourself, from a place of alignment.

- *Be impeccable with your word* → Speak up.
- *Don't take things personally* → Stay rooted in purpose, not ego.
- *Don't make assumptions* → Ask what's needed.
- *Always do your best* → Trust the impact of small, steady efforts.

Throughout history, we've seen sacred activism at work:

- Julian of Norwich wrote visions of divine love amidst plague and patriarchy.
- Harriet Tubman followed divine intuition to lead enslaved souls to freedom.
- Martin Luther King Jr. preached nonviolent revolution from a mountaintop of faith.
- Mother Teresa said, *"We can do no great things, only small things with great love."*

And in African Ubuntu philosophy: *"I am because we are."* Every act of healing, of service, of truth-telling, lifts the whole.

I-Thou: Seeing God in the Other

Martin Buber's *I-Thou* philosophy is sacred activism's lens: to see each person not as an object (an "It"), but as a divine presence (a "Thou").

When you treat someone as sacred, they rise. When you act as if they are God in disguise, the world begins to shift.

This takes form in practice.

- Look someone in the eyes.
- Listen with your whole body.
- Speak to their *soul*, not just their ears.
- Honor their dignity, even in disagreement.

In doing so, *you become the embodiment of sacred activism.* A walking prayer. A light-bearer. A revolution.

Rooting Purpose in the Present

Sacred activism isn't someday. It's now. It's local. It's daily.

Don't wait until you have a platform.
Don't wait until you're healed enough.
Don't wait until you're "ready."

Your story is already enough.
Your presence is already powerful.
Your love is already a revolution.

So the question is:
What will you *do* with it?

Begin With This:

The Ripple Act Ritual

At the start of each week, ask yourself:

"What sacred act can I offer from my soul this week?"

Write it down. Commit to it. Do it with love. No one else needs to see it.
But the universe will.

Because every sacred act matters.

Global Connection: The Thread of Oneness

There is no such thing as isolated healing. Your transformation does not exist in a vacuum. Every shift you make within yourself, every breath of peace, every act of courage, every layer of trauma transmuted, echoes outward. *That* is the thread of oneness.

Global connection is the spiritual technology of knowing:

"My light is not mine alone."

It is a frequency that weaves through Indigenous wisdom, quantum physics, mystic teachings, and modern science. Aboriginal Dreamtime wove every human, animal, and landform into a living songline of interdependence. Buddhist tonglen practice teaches us to breathe in the pain of others and transmute it with love. Neuroscience reveals that collective practices, like synchronized meditation, prayer, or even shared emotion, create coherence between human brainwaves, syncing hearts and minds across vast distances.

This is not a poetic metaphor. It's a bioelectromagnetic truth.

When you cry for justice in one corner of the world, someone across the globe feels an unexplainable resolve to rise. When you soften into love, you contribute to the planet's vibrational upgrade.

When you release your pain, you make space in the collective field for someone else to take their first breath of healing.

Your pain, once a point of separation, becomes a bridge, and your healing? It strengthens the tapestry we are all part of.

So stand under the stars tonight. Breathe deeply. Feel into your chest and know that your heartbeat is one pulse in the rhythm of seven billion. Every act you take, however quiet, is sacred global work.

Join a global meditation.

Whisper blessings to strangers as you pass them on the street.

Visualize your energy spreading like light threads across the globe, anchoring healing where darkness lingers.

You are not separate. You are the cosmic filament glowing through it all.

Shine as if your light *is the only light left*. Because sometimes, it is.

Your Ripple Is the Revolution

You came here for more than survival.

You came to rise. To ripple. To become a walking miracle who transforms others simply by existing in truth.

Your ripple is the revolution.

It doesn't start with a microphone or a million followers. It starts with the way you speak to your barista. The way you hold a stranger's gaze. The way you *forgive yourself* on a hard day and try again tomorrow.

Martin Buber's I-Thou reminds us: when we treat every human interaction as a meeting between divine equals, the mundane becomes miraculous. This presence, this reverence, rewires reality. When you see someone with love, you *invite* them to remember who they are. When you speak truth, you give permission for truth to exist in others.

Your scars? They are coordinates.
They mark the exact places where light broke through. They are proof you survived. Proof that you know the way out of the fire. And now, it is time to carry that light forward.

Modern psychology confirms what the mystics always whispered: your emotions are contagious. Mirror neurons don't just pick up facial expressions, they replicate *states of being*. Your joy, your compassion, your courage spreads. When you choose to heal, you give the collective nervous system a reason to exhale.

So stand tall.

Be the soul who smiles at chaos and anchors peace anyway.
Be the lighthouse on the cliff, unwavering in the storm.
Be the kind of presence that *feels* like home to those lost at sea.

It's about frequency.
It's about integrity.
It's about becoming a beacon, not by what you say, but by *who you are*.

You are not just healing.
You are the revolution.
One ripple at a time.

CHAPTER 14

Ignite Your Legacy – Crafting a Life of Impact

The fire you carry was never meant to stay in your chest. It was born to light the world.

Every betrayal, every ache, every sleepless night has become kindling. The fire is yours. And you, yes, you, are ready to step into it.

This is your moment.
Not to linger in pain's echo,
Not to rehearse the story of what broke you, but to *rise*.

This is your metamorphosis.
The embers of your wounds now fuel a flame so fierce, so divine, that even the heavens pause to witness it. You are no longer just the survivor, you are the torchbearer, the one who turns pain into purpose and makes the dark a little less dark for those who come after.

You've done the sacred work.
You've faced the shadow, healed the child, humbled the ego, and surrendered to the void. You've reclaimed your mind, your energy, your body, your soul. And now? You've arrived at the sacred crossroads, the moment all heroes face:

Will I stay safe and small, or will I become a force of transformation?
Will I hoard the light, or will I use it to ignite others?

Will I stay the victim?

This chapter is not a gentle invitation.
It's a *summons*.
A *clarion call* to build a legacy, it is our soul's assignment.
Your legacy is the energetic residue of your healing, how your existence alters the collective vibration. How your love, your story, your creation becomes a bridge for others to find their own light.

And no, it doesn't happen by chance.
It happens by design.
By choosing to live with radical intention, alchemizing pain into art, turning forgiveness into fuel, and answering the question: "How can I serve?"

In this chapter, we'll trace the path from trauma's ashes to eternal flame. We'll explore the science of epigenetics, how your healing writes new code into your DNA, and the psychology of purpose, revealing how meaning rewires your brain. We'll look at spiritual teachings that see legacy as a soul etched into time.

And you'll remember:

Your pain was never your punishment.
It was your *permission*.

To rise.
To serve.
To set the world on fire.

Naming the Flame: Trauma as the Spark of Transformation

Your journey began with a sacred act of courage: naming your pain.

Not hiding it.
Not sugarcoating it.
Not bypassing it with positivity and pretending you were "fine."

But *seeing it*. Facing it. Speaking it aloud.

Those raw wounds of betrayal, abandonment, heartbreak, and fear, whether carved into your childhood or freshly bleeding from adult moments, were once the storylines that defined you. But naming your trauma was never about glorifying your suffering. It was never about becoming the pain. It was about reclaiming your pen, taking authorship, and saying, *"This story bends toward light, and I'm the one turning the page."*

To name your trauma is to pull it out of the subconscious swamp where it distorts your choices, shapes your relationships, and hijacks your self-worth. It's bringing it into the light where it can be *understood*, *alchemized*, and *healed*.

And that naming? That was your first act of power.
It was your refusal to let pain become the author of your life.

Instead, you chose to write again, with intention, with dignity, and with truth.

Science Confirms: Purpose Rewrites the Script

Psychology's self-determination theory teaches us that we thrive through autonomy, mastery, and purpose. When we name our trauma and begin aligning with our deepest values, we shift from reactive survival to proactive creation. We stop coping and we begin *crafting*.

Naming trauma helps you understand its shape:

- Was it acute, a moment of rupture that shattered your sense of safety?
- Was it chronic, a slow erosion of your worth over years?
- Was it personal, passed down from family?
- Or collective, inherited through ancestral pain or social injustice?

Whatever the form, naming it was your way of saying:
"This stops with me."

There will still be days when old narratives sneak in.
Days when you feel the old pull of victimhood, where the inner voice says, "See? You'll never be more than what happened to you."
But now, you know better.

Breathe in.
Exhale slowly.

Your pain is not your identity.
It is the raw material of your becoming.

It is the soot that fertilizes the phoenix's rebirth.
It is the ember that sparks the torch you now carry for others.

Channeling the Current: Turning Wounds Into Wisdom

Let's talk about how far we've come since you started reading this book:

Energy work became your crucible, the sacred container where trauma's heavy embers were no longer buried but transmuted into light. This wasn't just healing. It was alchemy. The moment you decided to stop fearing your pain and start *working with it*, you entered a sacred laboratory, one where ancient spiritual truths and modern science finally shook hands.

Your pain, once a chaotic storm, became a current you could learn to *channel*. No longer drowning in emotion, you became the riverbed, directing the flow, guiding the surge.

You began to feel the hum of life force moving through your body, like a forgotten language suddenly remembered. Visualization. Breathwork. Grounding. Bare feet on the earth. Shaking. Stillness. These weren't just trendy practices. They were energy work. Conversations between your nervous system and the divine.

Quantum physics teaches us that everything is vibration, including your thoughts, your cells, your trauma. What you think, feel, and focus on shifts your vibrational frequency and, in turn, your energetic reality. Just like a radio, you had to tune yourself to a new station to receive a different song.

And inside your cells? Mitochondria, the powerhouses of life, respond to the frequencies you embody. Stress contracts them. Peace and purpose expand them. When you aligned with love, breath, truth, and presence, your biology literally began to repair. You weren't just changing your mood. You were rewriting your operating system.

Epigenetics, the study of how experiences influence gene expression without changing DNA, offers a biological framework for understanding how stress, nourishment, belief, and behavior leave molecular marks on the body. We've referenced this research throughout the book because it reshapes how we think about inheritance and healing. *Epigenetics confirms it*: your conscious choices, what you eat, think, believe, and do, can influence the way your genes express themselves. You're not doomed by DNA. You are sculpting your lineage in real time. Your healing ripples backward to your ancestors and forward to your children. That's not a metaphor. That's science and soul in one.

This is where science becomes sacred and breath becomes prayer.

You learned not to run from pain, but to listen to it. To honor it. To *alchemize* it. You discovered that grief is not a curse, it's a compass. That anger is sacred fuel. That trauma is not your identity, it's your invitation to step into power.

And in that shift, you became your own healer.

So the next time doubt whispers, or pain surges, don't panic.

Stand still. Root deep. Tune in.
You know how to ride the current now.

The Fire of Forgiveness: Alchemizing Self-Love

Self-love and forgiveness were the sacred flames that purified your heart, transmuting old wounds into radiant light. Cleansing the residue of shame, guilt, and resentment with the fiercest love of all: your own.

This wasn't about forgetting. It wasn't about pretending nothing happened or spiritually bypassing your scars. It was about *releasing the grip* pain had on your identity. Forgiveness became your liberation, a soul-deep decision to no longer carry what was never yours to hold. Claiming your power back.

You began to cradle your own soul the way you once wished someone else would. Whispering, "I am enough," is a radical vow. A sacred reclamation. A warrior's love letter to their wounded self.

And in that moment, something shifted.

Forgiveness of others became easier, not because they deserved it, but because *you did*. You deserved peace. You deserved lightness. You deserved to stop letting the actions of the unhealed keep their grip on your nervous system. You learned to see those who hurt you as mirrors of their own pain, *still accountable*, but no longer defining *you*.

This isn't about absolving abuse or excusing harm. It's about refusing to become a vessel for their shadow. As you stood in the fire, something profound occurred: your pain became your teacher, not your identity.

In those moments of flow (writing, dancing, loving, creating) you entered a state of divine rhythm where your soul aligned with truth. Time dissolved. Doubt faded. You remembered who you were beneath the ache: A creator. A channel. A vessel of sacred light.

If guilt still lingers, if shame sometimes creeps back in, let it. Acknowledge it. Smile at it. Those feelings are echoes, not truths. Your true frequency is love.

Psychology calls it reappraisal. Mystics call it transmutation. Neuroscience calls it integration. You can call it coming home.

And here's the truth that can't be shaken:
Your past is not your prison. It's your prologue.
Your scars are not shameful. They are signatures of survival.
They are proof you've walked through fire, and *didn't burn*.
You *became the fire*.

Interlude: While Writing This Chapter...

Let me pull the curtain back for a moment.

As I sit here writing this very chapter, on forgiveness, self-love, and the radiant path forward, I am still healing. Not from the echoes of childhood pain or trauma learned from life lessons that carved scars into my subconscious, but from *right now* pain. Present pain. The kind that clutches your chest at night and settles in your stomach like a boulder you can't quite move.

I am grieving a breakup with the love of my life. A man I believed I'd build a future with. A man I still miss every morning, every evening, and sometimes in the middle of a sentence I'm writing to you. And it *hurts.* In my chest. In my bones. In the fragile ache of being human.

So when I speak of transmuting pain into light, know this: I'm not preaching from some healed mountaintop. I'm walking through fire *with you.* Writing this book *is* my healing. My offering. My way of facing the imprint that past wounds left on my relationships, my trust, and the way I sometimes brace for abandonment even in safe places.

But even now, even through tears that fall at this very moment, I choose to stand for myself. I choose *self-love over self-sacrifice.* I choose *boundaries over begging.* I choose *truth over fantasy.* And I choose to *write this book*, not as a perfected being, but as a woman who still believes in love, in healing, in growth, even through heartbreak.

So if you're here, wondering why it still hurts, why it still feels heavy, even after all the work, know this:

You are allowed to ache.
You are allowed to miss them.
And you are *still* allowed to rise.

You are not a failure because you feel. You are a *miracle* because you continue. Every breath you take in the midst of grief is an act of defiance against the lie that you're too broken to heal.

Your softness is not your weakness. It's your *access point* to compassion. Your empathy is not a curse, it's your magic. And you do *not* have to wait until you are "fully healed" to help others or to become the light.

I don't have all the answers. But I do have this truth: *Healing hurts. But it frees.*
And if you stay with it, if you choose yourself, *the ache will fade.* Slowly. Gently. Day by day. And one day, your breath won't catch in your throat when you think of them. One day, your joy will outweigh the grief.

And until then, I'll walk with you.
We're not perfect, we're just powerful in our willingness to try.

Legacy Embodied: From Flame to Impact

You've walked through fire and emerged not as ashes, but as *alchemy*.

The light you carry now isn't borrowed. It's earned. It was forged in grief, clarified in truth, and sealed in the silence of sleepless nights where you chose to heal instead of harden.

This light, *your* light, is no longer a secret sanctuary. It's a torch. A beacon. A guide for others who are still navigating their own darkness.

Your pain, once private and paralyzing, is now a map. A compass, etched with empathy, lined with scars, and pointing toward collective healing. You are a healer because you've turned every fracture into a window where light gets in, and *out*.

This is what it means to *embody your legacy*.

Søren Kierkegaard called it the "leap of faith", the moment when you stop waiting for certainty and choose purpose anyway. That leap is your legacy: a decision to become a lighthouse when it's still storming. To live as a beacon, not a shadow. Not just for yourself, but for everyone watching you silently from the shore, wondering if it's safe to rise.

Let this land in your body: Legacy is not built in grand speeches or final moments. It's carved in the everyday, when you return a call you've been avoiding, when you forgive someone who'll never apologize, when you choose to love *without losing yourself again*.

It's in the moment you say *no* with grace, *yes* with clarity, and *I'm healing* with power. It's when you *choose not to shrink*, even when it would be easier.

Stand under the stars. Breathe. Let your spine lengthen, your heart steady. Say aloud:

"My pain is my purpose. My legacy begins now."

And mean it.

Let your presence be felt long after the room is empty, because your energy lingered with intention, because your story cracked someone else open, because your courage gave someone else permission to breathe again.

Legacy is *not* what you leave behind when you're gone.
It's what you *awaken while you're here.*

The Eternal Flame: You Are the Living Legacy

Your legacy is an eternal blaze, one that crackles across time, across souls, reshaping the emotional climate of this world with every heart it illuminates.

Every trauma you've named, every wound you've stitched with truth, every drop of sweat from the sacred labor of healing, these are *sparks*. They are the kindling that feeds the fire of your legacy.

And this fire doesn't die with you.

It *lives through others*. Through the child you raised with more tenderness than you received. Through the friend you held during their storm. Through the art you made when you thought you had nothing left to give. Through the truth you spoke when your voice trembled. Through the silence you offered instead of judgment. *Through the boundaries you held in honor of your growth.*

Kierkegaard's leap of faith still calls: the moment you stop begging for permission from life and choose to *ignite* it instead. Faith in your purpose is not a passive belief. It's a *radical refusal* to let pain have the final word.

Let this land softly, yet powerfully:

You are a survivor.
You are powerful.
You were born to *light the way.*

Your healing is a planetary mission.

It echoes. It multiplies. It expands. And what once felt like a solitary ache becomes the revolution of a million softened hearts.

Legacy.

So, don't shrink now.

Leave footprints made of fire and compassion. Walk through this world as a living invocation: a prayer that breathes, a light that lingers.

So go on. Ignite it all. Ignite it with purpose. Ignite it with truth.
Ignite it because *you dared to heal.*
And because the world needs your flame now more than ever.

CHAPTER 15

Navigating the Inner Storm – Healing Severe Mental Illness

This chapter is a quiet harbor, a sacred space for those who live with minds that feel like warzones. Not just fleeting sadness or occasional worry, but chronic, clinical, consuming conditions, the kind that dig trenches in the psyche and make everyday life feel like an uphill climb through fog, fire, and silence.

If your mind has felt heavy with depression, hijacked by anxiety, fractured by schizophrenia, or tossed between highs and lows with bipolar disorder, this space is for you.

And for those who love someone in the eye of these storms, this space is yours too. Because walking beside someone through mental illness takes a strength the world rarely recognizes. The Glow Up Project is not only for those doing the inner work, but also for those *holding space when someone else can't yet hold themselves.*

We've spent this journey naming trauma, awakening spirit, and stepping boldly into our radiance. But this is where we pause, to honor the truth, that some wounds run deeper than mantras can reach. Some storms are neurological. Chemical. Generational. Invisible to the outside world and yet seismic within.

And that doesn't mean you are helpless. It means your healing may require *more tools, more support,* and *more time.* And that is *okay.*

This chapter is not a promise to cure, but a commitment to care. It's about walking with compassion through the darkest corners of the psyche, with a flashlight of science in one hand and the steady warmth of soul in the other.

A Note of Care and Integrity

Before we continue, I want to be clear about the spirit and scope of this chapter. I am not a psychiatrist, psychologist, or medical doctor, and nothing

What I offer here comes from lived experience, deep study, and years of navigating relationships with people living with severe mental illness, as well as learning how to protect my own nervous system, boundaries, and heart along the way. The insights shared are grounded in widely accepted psychological and neurological research, paired with a compassionate, trauma-informed perspective.

If you or someone you love is struggling with severe mental illness, professional support is essential. This chapter is meant to support understanding, reduce shame, and offer relational guidance, not to stand alone, but to walk alongside proper care.

You deserve help. You deserve safety. You deserve dignity.

Your storm is not your story. It's the forge where your resilience is born.

This journey is different.

Let's walk gently here.
Let's speak clearly.
Let's hold the impossible truths and still believe in possibility.

Because you are worth healing. Even when it feels impossible. Especially then.

The conditions we're addressing here are not merely passing clouds, they are full hurricanes that alter the landscape of one's identity and perception.

These conditions, clinical depression, narcissistic personality disorder (NPD), antisocial personality disorder (ASPD), schizophrenia, bipolar disorder, and severe anxiety disorders, are not simply emotional struggles. They involve complex neurological, physiological, and psychological processes that shape perception, behavior, and identity.

They twist time, memory, connection, and even language. Some people feel every moment of the struggle and are fighting to find a way forward; others may not yet recognize the storm within, and that's okay, this chapter is for both the seeker and the soul who stands beside them.

We'll explore each condition with honesty and reverence, offering insights into what it feels like from the inside and what can be done to foster healing or meaningful support. There are no simple fixes, but there is hope. There are steps. There is connection.

What follows is not theory from a distance, it is perspective forged through proximity, research, and the lived reality of loving people inside these storms. As philosopher Karl Jaspers once said, "in the depths of despair, we find the call to exist authentically."

That is what this is, an invitation to keep showing up.

But before we move on, I need to tell you something from my heart.

I'm not writing this chapter from a mountaintop of enlightenment, waving a magic wand over someone else's pain. I'm writing this from the trenches.

I know what it's like to live with the daily psychological warfare of someone who twists your truth until you question your own sanity. I spent years in a marriage where gaslighting wasn't a rare tactic, it was the daily norm. Where emotional abuse was masked as charm to the outside world, and every boundary I tried to build was torn down with manipulation, cruelty, or control.

Even years after divorce, I'm still navigating the wreckage, through courts, co-parenting battles, ongoing harassment, and the painful attempts to protect my children from the same cycles I've worked so hard to heal.
Some days, it feels like the storm is still raging.

Romantic relationships have been hard. Healing while someone keeps trying to drag you back into the trauma isn't just exhausting, it's *suffocating*.
But I'm still here. Writing. Healing. Learning how to forgive what feels unforgivable. How to love through fear. How to raise strong children

while I myself rebuild.
And I'm doing it with you.

This chapter is not a solution, it's a lifeline.
It's for anyone who's felt trapped in a loop of mental illness, your own, or someone else's, and is desperate to find footing again.

I am walking this too.
Not perfectly.
But honestly.
And that's where healing begins.

Clinical Depression: Finding Light in the Void

Clinical depression is not just sadness, it is an existential gravity. It is the numb ache behind your eyes, the invisible weight in your limbs, the thick fog that erases color from the world. It is the feeling of being hollow and heavy at the same time, as though you're trapped in a soundproof room screaming for help that no one can hear.

Some days, it feels like you're moving underwater. Like brushing your teeth is a heroic act. Like answering a simple text is an impossible task. You may forget what joy feels like, not because you're ungrateful, but because the connection to it has been chemically or neurologically short-circuited.

Let's be very clear: Depression is *not* laziness. It is *not* a lack of gratitude.
It is an illness; real, diagnosable, treatable.
And most dangerously, it *lies to you in your own voice.*

The Science Behind the Shadows

Clinical depression affects the brain's chemistry, circuitry, and communication. It is often driven by a combination of:

- Neurotransmitter imbalance, particularly in serotonin, dopamine, and norepinephrine.
- Chronic stress and trauma, which alter the HPA (hypothalamic-pituitary-adrenal) axis, creating ongoing cortisol dysregulation.

- Inflammation and immune dysregulation, with studies now linking depression to elevated inflammatory markers like CRP and cytokines.
- Gut-brain axis disruption, where poor microbiome diversity can affect serotonin production (about 90% of serotonin is made in the gut).
- Epigenetics, where unresolved trauma from prior generations may alter how your genes express emotional regulation and stress responses.

This is not just "in your head", it's in your *biology*. But biology is not destiny. And hope lives in your next breath.

If You Are Living With It: Gentle, Grounded Guidance

Healing from depression doesn't require you to leap, it requires you to *inch*. And every inch matters.

- Begin with micro-movements. Open one curtain. Drink one glass of water. Let the sun kiss your skin for 30 seconds. Celebrate it. These are not small victories, they are *seismic*.
- Breathe with intention. Try five deep belly breaths, letting your exhale be longer than your inhale. This signals your nervous system that you are safe, even when your mind doesn't agree.

Seek treatment that honors both science and soul:

- *Therapeutic tools*: Cognitive Behavioral Therapy (CBT), EMDR (for trauma-related depression), Internal Family Systems (IFS), or somatic therapies.
- *Medication*: Antidepressants like SSRIs or SNRIs can be life-saving for many, but always discuss with a trusted psychiatrist.
- *Nutrition*: Nutritional psychiatry is on the rise. Omega-3s, vitamin D, magnesium, zinc, B-complex vitamins, and amino

acids like tryptophan or tyrosine can support neurochemical balance. A functional medicine doctor or integrative psychiatrist can help assess.
- *Movement & light*: Rebounding, gentle walks, and exposure to natural light or light therapy lamps have measurable effects on mood and circadian rhythm.

Depression lies, but your effort is the truth. Every time you show up, even to this page, you are defying gravity.

If You Are Loving Someone With Depression

You cannot fix them.
But you can sit beside them without judgment, and that may change everything.

- Say less, hold more. Don't offer platitudes like "Just think positive." Instead, say:
  "I'm here. I'm not going anywhere. I don't need you to be okay to be worthy of love."
- Learn about their condition, through books, videos, or support groups, so your compassion has roots.
- Offer actionable help, not abstract advice:
  - *"Want me to bring you dinner?"*
  - *"Want to go for a 5-minute walk and say nothing?"*
  - *"Would you feel better if I stayed on the phone while you take your meds?"*
- Celebrate the tiniest wins: getting dressed, making a call, washing a dish. To someone with depression, those are mountains moved.
- Honor your limits too. Supporting someone with depression can be draining. You must care for your own nervous system, too, and know when to call in professionals.

Your Light Is Not Lost, It's Just Dimmed

Depression is a thief. It tries to steal your past, your joy, your worth.
But it cannot steal your *truth*.
You are *still here*. That alone is proof of your strength.

Even in your darkest hour, there is a part of you reading this, *seeking healing, seeking light.* That part is still alive. And that part is enough to build from.

Let's honor that.
One breath. One step. One truth at a time.

Narcissistic Personality Disorder (NPD): Softening the Walls

Narcissistic Personality Disorder is one of the most misunderstood and emotionally charged diagnoses, especially for those on the receiving end of its storms. It's easy to reduce it to arrogance, manipulation, or a lack of empathy. But beneath the surface of inflated self-importance often lies something far more fragile: a shattered sense of self, buried under layers of psychic armor.

This condition is not about vanity. It is about survival.

At the root of NPD is often a child who never felt unconditionally loved. Someone who learned, early and painfully, that worthiness came only through performance, perfection, or control. That being vulnerable meant being unsafe. And so, a mask was formed, a false self designed to protect against humiliation, abandonment, or the unbearable shame of not being enough.

Understanding the Wound Beneath the Mask

NPD isn't just behavioral, it's neurobiological and psychological:

- Psychologically, individuals may experience an internal tug-of-war between grandiosity and deep self-loathing. This fragile identity is constantly seeking external validation to hold it together, and any criticism, however small, can feel like a mortal wound.
- Neurobiologically, research suggests possible reduced gray matter in brain regions associated with empathy, emotional regulation, and self-reflection, particularly the anterior insula and prefrontal cortex.

- Developmentally, NPD is often linked to emotional neglect, conditional love, enmeshment with a narcissistic caregiver, or early psychological abuse. The child internalizes the belief: "I am only safe when I am impressive." Vulnerability becomes equated with annihilation.

This is why those with NPD often exhibit emotional defensiveness, control-seeking behavior, or manipulation, not necessarily because they are "evil," but because they are trying to avoid re-experiencing psychological death. It's tragic. And complex.

If You Are Living With NPD: A Path to Healing

If you recognize these patterns in yourself, first, know this: awareness is sacred. It's rare, and it's brave.

Healing from NPD doesn't require destroying who you are, it asks that you *excavate who you were before the armor*. Under the façade is a real, feeling human being. One worthy of love.

- Therapeutic tools like Schema Therapy, Internal Family Systems (IFS), and Psychodynamic Therapy can help reconnect you with the disowned parts of yourself.
- Journaling your emotional reactions, especially the ones that trigger defensiveness, can reveal old wounds asking for care.
- Begin practicing micromoments of empathy. Ask yourself in heated moments: "What might they be feeling?" This isn't about excusing others, it's about expanding your emotional map.
- Build slow, stable relationships with people who mirror your value while challenging your defenses. Safety grows over time. So does authenticity.

You don't have to be perfect. You just have to be willing to trade the illusion of invincibility for the reality of being deeply human.

If You Love Someone With NPD: Boundaries and Compassion

Being in a relationship with someone with NPD, whether romantic, familial, or co-parenting, can feel like walking on broken glass while holding your breath. The inconsistency, gaslighting, charm flips, and rage cycles can wreak havoc on your nervous system.

But here's the truth: you cannot heal them. And you are not responsible for their journey. You are only responsible for protecting your light.

- Set clear, non-negotiable boundaries. Write them down. Speak them calmly. Hold them fiercely.
- Avoid explaining your needs over and over, this often leads to emotional entrapment. Instead, act. Boundaries are not requests; they are realities.
- When they show vulnerability, respond *without rescuing*. Empathize, but don't enable. Try language like:
- "That sounds really painful. I hope you're able to explore that with someone safe."
- Encourage therapy, but not as an ultimatum. Instead, frame it as a door to freedom:

"This might help you feel less reactive, more in control, more at peace."

And most importantly: take care of your own nervous system. Get support. Trauma therapy, somatic experiencing, and education around narcissistic abuse can be life-changing. Your glow is not meant to be dimmed by someone else's fear of facing their own.

A Personal Note from Me to You

I know this pain intimately.

I lived through years in a mentally and emotionally abusive marriage with someone I now believe exhibited narcissistic, and possibly sociopathic, traits. Even after divorce, I still experience the fallout:

legal battles, co-parenting chaos, manipulative tactics aimed at destabilizing both me and my children. I know what it's like to love someone who can't, or won't, truly see you. To question your own sanity. To rebuild yourself in the rubble.

This chapter is not written from a pedestal.
It's written from a battlefield.
And if you're reading this while still inside the storm, let this be your reminder:

You are not crazy. You are not alone. And you are not powerless.

Healing from NPD, whether you have it, or you've loved someone who does, is a reclamation of *truth*. Of *reality*. Of *your right to peace*.

You don't need to become cold to be strong.
You just need to start protecting your own light with the same fierceness you once gave to saving theirs.

Antisocial Personality Disorder (ASPD): Finding a Path to Connection

ASPD is often painted as "the villain diagnosis," but let's strip the stigma. Many with ASPD have lived through unimaginable trauma. They may have developed emotional detachment as survival.

Insights: ASPD is marked by disregard for societal norms, impulsivity, and sometimes aggression or manipulation. However, many people with ASPD, or traits of it, function in the world, seek meaning, and desire connection. Studies show that early intervention can change the trajectory. Brain scans often reveal reduced activity in the prefrontal cortex (impulse control) and amygdala (emotional processing), but neuroplasticity tells us this can change.

Guidance for You: Begin with noticing impact. Ask, "What did my action cause in another?" Therapy with someone trained in personality disorders is essential. Group therapy can offer reality-checks and feedback in safe ways. Martial arts, meditation, or structure-based activities help train impulse control and bring back a sense of agency. You are not beyond love.

Guidance for Loved Ones: Hold hope, but don't hold the weight alone. Detachment with love is often required. Offer compassion without becoming a doormat. Provide honest feedback calmly, and honor their journey, even if from a distance.

Schizophrenia: Reclaiming Your Reality

Schizophrenia is often feared, but it is not a death sentence, it's a neurological condition that alters perception. It may involve hallucinations, delusions, disorganized speech, or cognitive decline.

Insights: Schizophrenia has strong genetic and biological roots, dopamine and glutamate dysregulation play a key role. Brain imaging often shows differences in hippocampal volume and connectivity. But medication, therapy, and structure can provide profound improvement. People with schizophrenia are often deeply sensitive, creative, and intelligent.

Guidance for You: Find a consistent psychiatric provider. Medication adherence is crucial to managing psychosis, and side effects should be discussed, not feared in silence. Routine is your best friend, sleep hygiene, nutrition, movement. Art therapy, grounding exercises, and spiritual connection (through safe, structured practices) can bring meaning and dignity.

Guidance for Loved Ones: Do not argue with delusions, redirect with love. Create calm, structured environments. Show up with consistency and predictability. Speak clearly and lovingly. Learn the early signs of psychosis relapse. Your faith in their potential is a lightpost.

Bipolar Disorder: Balancing the Tides of Light and Shadow

Bipolar disorder is not simply a swing between high and low, it is the exhausting dance between wildfire and undertow. It's fire and water trying to occupy the same body. It's flight followed by freefall. The mania or hypomania can feel like divine momentum: ideas flowing faster than time, energy surging through your veins. And then, crash.

The lows come like waves that pull you under. Heavy. Silent. Devastating.

Insights: Understanding the Bipolar Brain

There are two primary types:

- Bipolar I involves full manic episodes, often intense enough to require hospitalization or result in risky behaviors.
- Bipolar II includes hypomania, a milder but still potent elevation in mood and energy, followed by often-debilitating depressive episodes.

Across both types, depressive symptoms often last longer and feel more familiar, while the elevated states can feel seductive or surreal.

Biologically, bipolar disorder is linked to:

- Disrupted circadian rhythms (your internal clock), which is why sleep patterns are a major trigger and stabilizer.
- Dysregulation in the limbic system, the brain's emotional center, particularly the amygdala and prefrontal cortex, which affect mood regulation and decision-making.
- Mitochondrial dysfunction and oxidative stress may also play a role, hinting at cellular energy imbalances, your very power supply flickering unpredictably.

Episodes can be triggered by:

- Sleep deprivation
- Seasonal changes (especially spring or fall)
- Substance use
- Life transitions or unregulated stress

Guidance for You: Living Within Your Rhythm

Living with bipolar disorder is about learning to honor your tides. It's not about avoiding every wave, it's about learning to surf them with grace and strategy.

- Track your moods with a journal or an app. Noticing patterns can alert you to oncoming shifts.
- Create a structured daily routine: consistent wake/sleep times, balanced meals, exercise. These aren't just good habits, they're medicine for your nervous system.
- Medication is not a failure, it's often a lifeline. Mood stabilizers like lithium, lamotrigine, or atypical antipsychotics like quetiapine can create the neurological balance needed to build a life that feels like yours. Always under a doctor's supervision and recommendation.
- Therapeutic support is crucial, CBT, DBT, and psychoeducation can help you recognize triggers, reframe thoughts, and regulate behaviors.
- Build a "crisis plan": identify warning signs, coping tools, emergency contacts, and safe spaces. This is self-protection, not pessimism.

Guidance for Loved Ones: Loving Through the Seasons

Loving someone with bipolar disorder can feel like trying to map shifting tides.

Don't romanticize the highs or demonize the lows. Avoid saying things like "I miss your energy" during manic phases or "Why can't you just try harder?" in the lows. These words wound.

Help create structure, not force it. "Want to go for a walk at 8?" is different than "You should really be getting up earlier."

Use calm, grounding language:

- "I love you through every season."
- "I see your effort, even when you can't feel it."
- "You are not your episode."

Let them know they are safe to feel both their fire and their frost. Educate yourself. Understand the phases. This helps you respond, not react.

Severe Anxiety Disorders: Easing the Relentless Grip

Anxiety doesn't whisper, it *screams* through the nervous system, hijacking your peace like an alarm that won't stop blaring. It isn't just "worrying too much." It's trembling hands that can't hold a cup of tea. It's chest tightness in the grocery aisle. It's the unshakable sense that something is *wrong*, even in moments of safety. It's the one I know best and have personally delt with.

And while it may feel like your mind is betraying you, anxiety is not your enemy, it's your system overfiring to protect you, long after the threat is gone.

Insights: The Brain in Overdrive

Anxiety disorders show up in many forms:

- Generalized Anxiety Disorder (GAD): chronic tension, hypervigilance, catastrophizing.
- Panic Disorder: sudden episodes of intense fear, chest pain, breathlessness, derealization.
- Social Anxiety: fear of judgment, avoidance of interaction, physical symptoms in public settings.
- Phobias: intense, irrational fears tied to specific objects or situations.
- Obsessive-Compulsive Disorder (OCD): intrusive thoughts (obsessions) + repetitive behaviors (compulsions) as coping mechanisms.

All of them share a common biological thread: a hypersensitive amygdala, the brain's fear center, and a dysregulated HPA axis (hypothalamic-pituitary-adrenal), the system that controls your stress response.

Long-term anxiety can lead to:

- Cortisol dysregulation
- Adrenal fatigue

- Digestive issues (via gut-brain axis dysfunction)
- Sleep disruption
- Memory and focus problems

But there is hope. The brain's neuroplasticity means that even deeply ingrained anxiety patterns can be *retrained*, you can rewire the way your mind interprets the world.

Guidance for You: Reclaiming Calm, One Signal at a Time

You are not "too sensitive."
You are not "overreacting."
You are someone whose nervous system is trying to keep you alive, even when there's no immediate danger.

Let's show it that peace is safe.

Here's how:

- Cognitive Behavioral Therapy (CBT): teaches you to identify anxious thoughts and challenge them with truth.
- Exposure Therapy: gradually reintroduces you to feared situations in safe, supported ways.
- Vagus Nerve Resets: your vagus nerve is your calm switch. Activate it through:
    - Cold exposure (splash cold water on your face or use a cold compress)
    - Humming or chanting
    - Deep diaphragmatic breathing (try 4-7-8 breaths)
    - Laughter (yes, real or fake, it still works)

Nutritional Support:

- Avoid stimulants like caffeine (which spikes cortisol).
- Stabilize blood sugar with protein-rich meals and slow-release carbs.
- Ask your provider about L-theanine, magnesium glycinate, ashwagandha, omega-3s, or adaptogens.

Tools that Interrupt the Spiral:

- Tapping/EFT: Emotional Freedom Technique combines physical tapping with affirmations.
- Sensory kits: Ground with a scent (lavender), a touch (smooth stone), or sound (calm playlist).
- Meditation apps: Insight Timer, Calm, or Breathwork.

You are being called to *remember your calm.* And every moment you reach for peace, no matter how small, is a win.

Guidance for Loved Ones: Supporting Without Smothering

Anxious minds don't need fixing. They need safety.

Here's how to love someone through anxiety:

- Believe them. Don't say "Just relax" or "It's all in your head." Instead say:

  "I know this feels really real. I'm here with you."

- Co-regulate. Sit beside them. Breathe slowly so they can mirror you.
- Use grounding tools together. "Want to do a breath with me?" or "Try holding this cold stone."
- Respect their boundaries. If crowds, bright lights, or surprise events are triggers, don't force them to "get over it."
- Model peace. Stay grounded and calm. Avoid high-energy reactions or invalidation.

You are not their therapist, but your presence can be *deeply therapeutic.*

A Note From Me, To You

As someone who lives with the echoes of trauma, as someone who has been gaslit and disoriented, and who still sometimes wakes up feeling that heaviness in her chest, I see you.

Anxiety isn't always healed in a day or even in a year. But each breath you choose with intention, each time you *stay* instead of run, each time you gently say "I'm safe," you shift your chemistry, your patterns, your life.

Let's be clear: You're not failing when anxiety shows up.
You're practicing every time you meet it with compassion instead of fear.

You are not a fragile thing, you are a warrior learning to soothe the beast inside.
And every moment you choose stillness in the storm, *you win.*

A Sacred Closing: You Are the Lighthouse in the Storm

This chapter is my promise to you.

Whether you're the one crawling through the fog of your own mind or the one sitting beside someone who can't yet see their own light, know this: *you are not alone.* Your pain, your exhaustion, your fire, your compassion, it's all part of a legacy of love and resilience that refuses to break.

You've just read through the hardest truths. You've faced the language of suffering that many don't understand. And maybe it's your language too. Maybe it's the silent scream you've been carrying, or the echo of someone else's torment living rent-free in your nervous system.

Let me say it clearly: You are not your diagnosis. You are not their disorder.

Martin Buber taught that the sacred lives in true connection, *I-Thou,* soul to soul. And what you're doing right now, being here, still breathing, still caring, still trying, is that sacred act. *Meeting life exactly where it is, with love in your heart and truth in your hands.*

You may not have all the answers, but you are showing up with intention. That is divine.

You may still tremble when you speak your truth, but trembling does not mean you're weak. It means you're alive.

And in a world so numb and fast and angry, being alive and tender is a revolutionary act.

Your storm is not your story, it's the forge where your resilience is born. You don't have to be fearless. You just have to be willing. Willing to rise, to rest, to reach, to forgive, to try again.

CHAPTER 16

Your Radiant Toolkit – A Sacred Guide to Healing All Wounds

You stand at the culmination of a journey through pain, resilience, and radiant rebirth, holding scars that tell stories of survival, some etched by fleeting insecurities, others carved by losses so profound that they defy words, and some borne of battles with a mind turned against itself.

This is your sacred manual, a summary, a radiant toolkit to heal every wound, from the quiet tremors of trust betrayed to the seismic grief of life-altering trauma and the relentless weight of severe mental illness.

Here, you'll find the tools to balance your energy, the electric current that binds body, mind, and spirit, transforming pain into a purpose that lights the world. This is no fleeting fix but a lifelong guide, weaving science, spirit, and a touch of defiant joy to rewire your being for resilience and radiance.

From Cognitive Behavioral Therapy to sound healing, mindful nutrition to generational legacy, each modality is a thread in your heart's eternal canvas, a testament to your power to heal and uplift others.

Rewiring the Mind: Cognitive Behavioral Therapy and Acceptance

Your thoughts can be a cage or a key, trapping you in cycles of doubt or unlocking paths to freedom.

Cognitive Behavioral Therapy (CBT) is your tool to rewrite the scripts of self-doubt, those whispers of "I'm not enough" that linger after betrayal or failure. CBT empowers you to examine these distorted beliefs, notice the patterns, and replace them with truths grounded in your worth. Over time, you create new neural pathways through the miracle of neuroplasticity.

When you catch a thought like, "I always mess up," pause. Ask: "Is that true? Is there evidence? Can I tell a new story?" Replace it with: "I made a mistake, but I am still learning. I am still worthy."

Acceptance and Commitment Therapy (ACT) complements CBT, inviting you to sit with the emotions you once ran from, grief, fear, shame, and choose actions aligned with your values, not your fear. It's not about silencing the storm, it's learning to row your boat through it.

These tools support common wounds like abandonment and insecurity, but they are also anchored in severe mental health struggles like anxiety, depression, and trauma-induced beliefs.

Remember, your mind is not your master; it's your canvas, ready to be repainted with purpose.

Releasing the Body: Somatic Healing and Breathwork

Trauma doesn't just haunt the mind, it lives in the body. It's in the clenching of your jaw, the pain in your hips, the tension in your shoulders. Somatic healing, rooted in polyvagal theory, helps you release trauma through physical movement, tremors, and breath. When you allow the body to move how it needs to, whether that's shaking, crying, or dancing, you allow the energy that's been trapped to finally flow free.

Some people try TRE (Tension and Trauma Releasing Exercises): lie on the floor, let your legs tremble, and breathe through it. Whisper to yourself, "My body is releasing what no longer belongs to me."

You don't have to understand it, just trust that your body remembers how to heal.

Breathwork, too, is a sacred key. The 4-4-8 pattern (inhale 4, hold 4, exhale 8) regulates your vagus nerve, shifts your nervous system out of fight-or-flight, and invites calm. These practices help ease everything from daily stress to the chronic muscle tension of PTSD or the hypervigilance of anxiety disorders.

Reprocessing the Past: EMDR and Controlled Psychedelics

Some trauma lives on in your nervous system like it happened yesterday. Eye Movement Desensitization and Reprocessing (EMDR) works by guiding your eyes side to side while recalling painful memories, helping your brain reprocess them and strip them of their emotional charge. It's not erasure, it's transformation.

For trauma too deep for words, controlled psychedelics like MDMA and psilocybin, in safe, clinical settings, have been shown to rewire neural networks and increase connectivity in the brain. These tools are emerging powerhouses in treating PTSD, complex trauma, and even severe depression and addiction.

If memories overwhelm, remember, your past is not your captor; it's a chapter you can rewrite with clarity. You're not reliving, you're reclaiming.

Vibrating to Freedom: Sound Healing

Sound is the universe made tangible. Frequencies like 432 Hz or 528 Hz are believed to activate healing and promote harmony. Singing bowls, gongs, chanting, binaural beats, they all shift your brainwaves into more peaceful states (alpha or theta), where deep healing occurs.

Sound healing is especially powerful for those with trauma, ADHD, or severe anxiety. Lie down, close your eyes, and let the frequencies wash over you. Your cells are listening. Your soul is tuning itself back into alignment.

When distraction pulls you, take heart, your energy is not chaos; it's a symphony, waiting to harmonize.

Connecting to the Divine: Spiritual Awakening Practices

Spirituality is your reminder that you are more than a body, more than a diagnosis, more than a story. Whether you connect to God, Source, ancestors, or the collective unconscious, practices like meditation, prayer, and gratitude rituals tether you to something infinite.

A simple practice: each morning, name three things you're grateful for. Light a candle. Say, "I am guided." These acts ignite the soul's GPS.

These practices offer meaning after betrayal, connection amidst depression, and hope during the darkest moments of mental illness. When disconnection looms, say a prayer, your spirit is not lost; it's a flame, burning bright in the divine's embrace.

Resetting the System: Vagus Nerve Stimulation

The vagus nerve is the master key of the nervous system. When stimulated, through breath, cold plunges, vibration, or tech devices like gammaCore, it resets your system from survival to serenity.

Use this when you feel dysregulated, numb, or panicked. Even humming or chanting activates your vagus nerve. Consistent stimulation improves HRV (heart rate variability), an important marker of resilience.

This tool bridges common and severe wounds, offering a tech-savvy edge to healing.

Nourishing the Body: Mindful Nutrition and Joyful Movement

Food is healing. Choose living, vibrant foods, berries, greens, salmon, cacao. Prepare meals with intention. Eat slowly. Whisper, "I feed my light."

Joyful movement is about celebration. Dance. Stretch. Walk barefoot on the grass. Move like you love yourself. These practices lift mood, reduce cortisol, and combat the numbness of depression.

Your body is not an afterthought, it's a sacred altar. Nourish it with love.

Adorning the Self: Intentional Self-Presentation

How you dress is energy work. Put on something that makes you feel powerful, beautiful, whole. Wear colors that uplift you. Adorn yourself with ritual.

This is not vanity, it's sovereignty. When your trauma tells you to shrink, your style becomes your stand. Honor yourself.

Sustaining the Glow: Daily Radiance Practices and Community Anchoring

Your glow requires devotion. Begin each day with breath, intention, and one act of kindness, for yourself or another. These are the sacred rhythms that sustain transformation.

Anchor in community. Join a circle, message a friend, share your story. You heal in relationship. You glow brighter when mirrored in others.

Passing the Light: Generational Legacy

Your healing echoes through generations. Teach your children to breathe, to speak their truth, to rest, to rise. Share your tools with your community, your lineage, your soul family.

This is your legacy, not just a healed self, but a healed line. A healed world. You are the ancestor someone has been praying for.

Levinas reminds us that every act of care is a sacred responsibility.

Your radiant toolkit is not just a collection of techniques, it's a sacred guide, a rebellion against suffering, a commitment to aliveness. Each tool, from CBT to EMDR, from prayer to movement, is a doorway back to wholeness.

This is your bible, your blueprint, your magic. Shine forever.

A Closing Note from My Heart to Yours

Thank you for walking this journey with me.
Thank you for being brave enough to look inward, to feel what hurts, and to begin the work of healing. That alone is extraordinary.

If you've made it here, you've already done something powerful, chosen yourself. Chosen to break cycles. To try again. To believe that something better is possible.

You don't need to be perfect. You don't need to have it all figured out. Just stay honest. Stay kind to yourself. Keep going.
Healing takes time. And you are allowed to take all the time you need.

Let your light be imperfect, inconsistent, wild, and holy.
Let it be yours.

Some days will feel expansive and full of hope. Others may feel like you're starting over. That's okay. This isn't a straight line, it's a spiral, a returning to deeper layers of yourself with more love, more awareness, more grace.

You are not too much. You are not behind. You are exactly where you're meant to be.

Every step you've taken toward healing, no matter how small, is a step toward freedom. Toward peace. Toward a life that feels like yours.

And you don't have to walk it alone.

The Glow Up Project is here to support you long after this book closes. It's a movement for soul-deep healing and high-frequency living, for those ready to reclaim their energy, rewrite their story, and rise.

Two powerful symbols have followed us on this journey: the butterfly and the hummingbird. Let them be your reminder.

The butterfly, messenger of transformation, teaches that becoming requires unraveling. That beauty is born not from perfection, but from surrender and rebirth.
The hummingbird, with its quiet strength and unmatched agility, shows us that grace and power are not opposites, they coexist. That joy, presence, and adaptability are sacred tools in your flight forward.

Keep their wisdom with you. Let them live in your rituals, your reflections, your rising.

I hope you'll stay connected.
We have work to do, beautiful, meaningful, life-giving work. Together.

I'm so proud of you.
And I'm so honored to be on this journey with you.

With all my heart,
MJ Grace

BIBLIOGRAPHY

Adelian, H., et al. "The Effect of Mindfulness-Based Stress Reduction (MBSR) on Resilience among Vulnerable Women." *BMC Women's Health* 21. Article 390. https://doi.org/10.1186/s12905-021-01390-6.

Alhawatmeh, H. N., et al. "The Benefits of Mindfulness Meditation on Trait Mindfulness, Perceived Stress, and Cortisol in Nursing Students." PMC.

Aly, S. S. M., et al. "Dietary Factors in Major Depressive Disorder." *Frontiers in Neuroscience* 14: 582853. https://doi.org/10.3389/fnins.2020.582853.

Arnsten, A. F. T. "Stress Signalling Pathways that Impair Prefrontal Cortex Structure and Function." *Nature Reviews Neuroscience* 10 (2009): 410–422. https://doi.org/10.1038/nrn2648

Bargh, John A., and Tanya L. Chartrand. "The Unbearable Automaticity of Being." *American Psychologist* 54, no. 7: 462–479. https://doi.org/10.1037/0003-066X.54.7.462.

Bargh, John A. "Losing Consciousness: Automatic Influences on Consumer Judgment, Behavior, and Motivation." *Journal of Consumer Research* 29, no. 2: 280–285. https://doi.org/10.1086/341577.

Bergson, Henri. *Creative Evolution*. Translated by Arthur Mitchell. Macmillan, 1911.

Borsini, A., et al. "Nutrition and Behavioral Health Disorders: Depression and Anxiety." *Nutrients* 13, no. 10: 3534. https://doi.org/10.3390/nu13103534.

Chin, B., et al. "Psychological Mechanisms Driving Stress Resilience: Mindfulness-Based Evidence." *Frontiers in Psychology*.

Decety, J. (1996). The neurophysiological basis of motor imagery. Behavioural Brain Research, 77(1–2), 45–52. https://doi.org/10.1016/0166-4328(95)00225-1

Draganski, B., et al. "Changes in Grey Matter Induced by Training." *Nature* 427, no. 6972 (2004): 311–312. https://doi.org/10.1038/427311a

Ekinci, O., et al. "Nutrition and Depression: A Review of the Current Evidence." *Clinical Nutrition ESPEN* 48: 1–10. https://doi.org/10.1016/j.clnesp.2022.02.005.

Galante, J., et al. "A Mindfulness-Based Intervention to Increase Resilience to Stress in University Students: The Mindful Student Study." https://doi.org/10.17863/CAM.17080.

Goddard, N. *The Power of Awareness*. DeVorss & Company.

Goyal, M., et al. "Meditation Programs for Psychological Stress and Well-Being." *JAMA Internal Medicine* 174, no. 3 (2014): 357–368.

Hassin, R. R. "Yes It Can: On the Functional Abilities of the Human Unconscious." *Perspectives on Psychological Science* 8, no. 2: 195–207.

Hawkins, D. R. Power vs. Force: The Hidden Determinants of Human Behavior. 3rd ed. Hay House, Inc., 2012.

Hölzel, B. K., et al. "Mindfulness Practice Leads to Increases in Regional Brain Gray Matter Density." *Psychiatry Research: Neuroimaging* 191, no. 1 (2011): 36–43.

Jeannerod, M. (2001). Neural simulation of action: A unifying mechanism for motor cognition. NeuroImage, 14(1), S103–S109. https://doi.org/10.1006/nimg.2001.0832

Jung, C. G. Psychology and Alchemy. Collected Works of C. G. Jung, vol. 12. 1953.

Kahneman, D. *Thinking, Fast and Slow*. Farrar, Straus and Giroux.

Kierkegaard, Søren. Concluding Unscientific Postscript to Philosophical Fragments.

Kolb, B., and R. Gibb. "Brain Plasticity and Behaviour in the Developing Brain." *Journal of the Canadian Academy of Child and Adolescent Psychiatry* 20, no. 4 (2011): 265–276.

Kwok, J. Y. Y., et al. "Effects of Meditation and Yoga on Anxiety, Depression, and Inflammation Biomarkers." PMC.

Ma, X., Yue, Z.-Q., Gong, Z.-Q., Zhang, H., Duan, N.-Y., Shi, Y.-T., and Wei, G.-X. "The Effect of Diaphragmatic Breathing on Attention, Negative Affect, and Cortisol Response to Stress in Healthy Adults." *Frontiers in Psychology* 8. Article 874. https://doi.org/10.3389/fpsyg.2017.00874.

McEwen, B. S., and J. H. Morrison. "The Brain on Stress: Vulnerability and Plasticity of the Prefrontal Cortex over the Life Course." *Neuron* 79, no. 1 (2013): 16–29. https://doi.org/10.1016/j.neuron.2013.06.028

Muscaritoli, M., et al. "The Impact of Nutrients on Mental Health and Well-Being: Insights from the Literature." *Frontiers in Nutrition* 8: 656047. https://doi.org/10.3389/fnut.2021.656047.

Oh, V. K. S., et al. "Mindfulness, Stress, and Resilience: Evidence from Psychological Research." *Journal of Behavioral Health*.

Pascoe, M. C., and Bauer, I. E. "Psychobiological Mechanisms Underlying the Mood and Health Benefits of Meditation: HPA Axis Modulation." *Psychoneuroendocrinology*.

Rauch, S. L., Shin, L. M., and Phelps, E. A. "Neurocircuitry Models of Posttraumatic Stress Disorder and Extinction: Human Neuroimaging Research." *Biological Psychiatry* 60, no. 4: 376–382. https://doi.org/10.1016/j.biopsych.2006.06.004.

Rogerson, O. "Effectiveness of Stress Management Interventions on Cortisol Regulation: A Systematic Review and Meta-Analysis." *Psychoneuroendocrinology*.

Ruiz, Don Miguel. The Four Agreements: A Practical Guide to Personal Freedom. Amber-Allen Publishing, 1997.

Seki, Y., et al. "Effects of Mindfulness-Based Interventions on Brain Structure and Function: A Meta-Analysis." *Biomedicines* 12, no. 11 (2023): 2613.

Shin, L. M., and Liberzon, I. "The Neurocircuitry of Fear, Stress, and Anxiety Disorders." *Neuropsychopharmacology* 35, no. 1: 169–191. https://doi.org/10.1038/npp.2009.83.

Tanaka, C., et al. "Impact of Continued Mindfulness Practice on Resilience and Stress Adaptation." *Psychiatric and Clinical Neurosciences.*

Wilson, T. D. Strangers to Ourselves: Discovering the Adaptive Unconscious. Belknap Press of Harvard University Press.

Zielińska, M. A., Łuszczki, E., and Dereń, K. "Dietary Nutrient Deficiencies and Risk of Depression: A Review." *Nutrients* 15, no. 4: 948. https://doi.org/10.3390/nu15040948.

Are you ready to take your Power Back?

If you do not reclaim your mind, it will be shaped by everything that hurt you.
If you do not heal your nervous system, it will keep reliving a past that is already over.
If you do not interrupt the pattern, you will pass it on.

Your pain is not random.
Your anxiety is not weakness.
Your exhaustion is not your identity.

It is inherited. Conditioned. Wired into your biology.
And it stops with you.

This is not self-help.
This is self-liberation.

Here, neuroscience meets the sacred. Trauma is decoded. Survival is dismantled. You will understand how your brain adapted to protect you and how to rewire it to empower you.

We do not escape the dark.
We transform it.

Pain into power.
Trauma into triumph.
Conditioning into conscious creation.

This is for the cycle breaker.
The pattern interrupter.
The one who refuses to hand their wounds to the future.

You will not leave these pages inspired.
You will leave changed.

Grounded in your body.
Clear in your mind.
Sovereign in your life.

When you elevate your internal frequency, your reality reorganizes.
When enough of us do this, the world shifts.

This is not about becoming better.

It is about becoming powerful.

If something inside you recognizes this,
it is because you are ready.

Let's take your Power Back.